WHY GOOD THINKING
Starts with
GOD

ENDORSEMENTS

"Human cognition requires a moral compass to guide our thinking and thinking justly. It is an excellent book that helps us think about our thinking biblically and why God is the important Foundation in understanding this wonderful and mysterious aspect of who we are as human beings."

—DR. VIDYA SAGAR ATHOTA, ASSOCIATE PROFESSOR
Discipline Coordinator: Management, HR, Sport & Rec Management
School of Law and Business

"Dr. Fyson described his book as a 'little book'; however, it is a substantial one in terms of its encompassing perspectives on theology, sociology, psychology, education, and many more in relation to *thinking*. I appreciate the book's core message, which explicitly states that good thinking starts from God, knows Him through Jesus Christ, and is led by the Holy Spirit. This message may not be readily understood by the secular world, yet it has the potential to prompt reflection and exploration. I sincerely pray that this 'little book' will bring a big impact, not only to the Christian community but also as an inspiration for others on *thinking*."

—DR. SAMUEL CHENG, PRINCIPAL
United Christian College (Kowloon East), HONG KONG

"The book *Why Good Thinking Starts With God: Thinking About Thinking* is a much needed piece of literature for both Christians and non-believers. For the Christian, it encourages them to look at life—whether in thought, word, or deed—from a biblical perspective. For the non-believer, it will open their eyes to view life more clearly if taken from a Christian perspective. Stephen Fyson has done an excellent job in alerting us to 'think about our thinking'; and in doing so, the book brings Colossians 3:2 into a clearer light: 'Set your minds on things that are above, not on things that are on earth.' Highly recommended."

—GREG BONDAR, NATIONAL DIRECTOR
Christian Voice Australia

"This book is going to be especially helpful in the world where thinking is no longer in the minds of people because Google and other platforms are thinking for people. People are no longer reading their Bible. If one does not read the Bible, it will be impossible for such person to think godly. This book will be the best guide to lead people to thinking. This book will be the best tool for Christian education. Christian education is so affected by this separation of the spiritual from thinking, to a point that Christians do not realize that the best mind is the mind of Christ and the best thinking can only happened when you are in Christ."

—DR. SAMSON MAKHADO, DIRECTOR EMERITUS
Association of Christian Schools International, Africa

"In his book *Why Good Thinking Starts with God: Thinking About Thinking*, Dr. Stephen Fyson constructs a mosaic of ideas that craftily has the reader contemplating their own thought processes and how they emanate from God. In this age where metacognitive thinking is spoken about and referred to often, Dr. Fyson skillfully points the reader back to God, His wisdom, and His Word. The topic of thinking about thinking is tackled from every perspective—philosophical, practical, historical, and current. It is extensively referenced with the works of renowned Christian philosophers such as C. S. Lewis and Christian Smith and a multitude of other writers. Dr. Fyson carefully structures this book into logical sections that relate thinking to the brain and neuroscience, character, consciousness, twenty-first century technology, learning theory, and, penultimately, to faith. I recommend this book to those who may enjoy Christian philosophy in a very readable form."

—PETER KILGOUR, ASSOCIATE PROFESSOR
B.A. DipEd., G. Dip. EdAdmin, MEd, Maths EdD, MACE
Dean of Research
Avondale University

THINKING ABOUT THINKING

WHY GOOD THINKING *Starts with* GOD

DR. STEPHEN J. FYSON

Ambassador International
GREENVILLE, SOUTH CAROLINA & BELFAST, NORTHERN IRELAND
www.ambassador-international.com

WHY GOOD THINKING STARTS WITH GOD
THINKING ABOUT THINKING

©2024 by Dr. Stephen J. Fyson
All rights reserved

ISBN: 978-1-64960-429-3, paperback
eISBN: 978-1-64960-477-4

Cover Design by Karen Slayne
Interior Typesetting by Dentelle Design
Edited by Katie Cruice Smith and Megan Griffin

No part of this publication may be reproduced, distributed, or transmitted in any form or by any means, including photocopying, recording, or other electronic or mechanical methods, without the prior written permission of the publisher, except in the case of brief quotations embodied in critical reviews and certain other noncommercial uses permitted by copyright law. For permission requests, contact the publisher using the information below.

Unless otherwise noted, Scriptural quotations are taken from The Holy Bible, English Standard Version. ESV® Text Edition: 2016. Copyright © 2001 by Crossway Bibles, a publishing ministry of Good News Publishers..

Scripture marked MSG taken from The Message, Copyright © 1993, 2002, 2018 by Eugene H. Peterson

Scripture marked NKJV taken from the New King James Version®. Copyright © 1982 by Thomas Nelson. Used by permission. All rights reserved.

Scripture marked NIV taken from Holy Bible, New International Version®, NIV® Copyright ©1973, 1978, 1984, 2011 by Biblica, Inc.® Used by permission. All rights reserved worldwide.

Titles may be purchased in bulk for education, business, fundraising, or sales promotional use. For information, please email sales@emeraldhouse.com.

AMBASSADOR INTERNATIONAL	AMBASSADOR BOOKS
Emerald House	The Mount
411 University Ridge, Suite B14	2 Woodstock Link
Greenville, SC 29601	Belfast, BT6 8DD
United States	Northern Ireland, United Kingdom
www.ambassador-international.com	www.ambassadormedia.co.uk

The colophon is a trademark of Ambassador, a Christian publishing company.

ACKNOWLEDGMENTS

THE FOLKS AT AMBASSADOR INTERNATIONAL have been so helpful in making this little book more cohesive, better expressed, and more readable. Thank you to Anna, Katie, and Megan and the rest of the team!

I also want to recognize and acknowledge my fellow Christian psychologists in Australia, who have listened to me shape these ideas over the years. The hundreds of students I have taught in Christian schools and colleges have also been patient as I tried to find the language to make sense of the truths we find in the Bible about our minds and thoughts.

And in particular, there was a young lady about fifty years ago who started to listen to me explore the realities of unseen aspects of life—our spirituality—as it applied to our minds and life. Four years later, we were married; and she has maintained that patient and listening ear for over forty-five years. Thank you, Sandie!

TABLE OF CONTENTS

Acknowledgments   vii

Author's Note   1

CHAPTER 1
THINKING AND THE BIBLE   5

CHAPTER 2
THINKING AND CONSCIOUSNESS   31

CHAPTER 3
THINKING AND THE BRAIN   45

CHAPTER 4
THINKING AND CHARACTER   61

CHAPTER 5
THINKING AND LEARNING   81

CONCLUSION
THINKING AND FAITH   109

Bibliography   115

For Further Reading   121

About the Author   123

AUTHOR'S NOTE

HAVE YOU EVER BEEN IN a discussion (or debate) about why we or others do what we do? It sometimes goes along the lines of, "Well, he couldn't help it—just look at his family life." Or this apparent empathy might be expressed from a different angle: "You know, it is built into her. Haven't you heard of her diagnosis?" In recent times, it can be expressed as, "I was just born this way!" Or, in contrast, "It was what happened to me at home—I had no choice!"

All these ideas to help understand our choices are just that—ideas. But from where do they come? Are they all predetermined from our genetic capacities and predispositions? Do these ideas come from our social contexts, past and present? Or is something else happening? What are some of the implications of this aspect of reality if we are a Christian in the Western world?

For example, some social philosophers have claimed that we are in a therapeutic age.[1] Others have noted that we are in age of "emotivism" or "expressivism."[2] Still others have noted that our

---
1   Philip Rieff, *The Triumph of the Therapeutic: Uses of Faith After Freud* (Wilmington: ISI Books, 2007).
2   Alasdair MacIntyre, *After Virtue: A Study in Moral Theory, Third Edition* (Notre Dame: University of Notre Dame Press, 2007).

secular age has resulted in an increase of "me-ism" that is focused on "safetyism"[3] and that this self-focus hides behind a distorted science called "scientism" within a declining commitment toward personal responsibility.[4]

That is what this little book is about. It is not an exhaustive treatment of the topic. That would be a very different kind of creature! Instead, it invites you to take a seat, relax, and think about thinking. The propositions outlined in these pages will ask you to celebrate that even though we have much in common with animals, we are distinctly different. It asks you to wonder at our minds being much more than our brains. It will suggest that there are clear signposts that invite you to freshly see that thinking as a human being is inherently spiritual. And it will also challenge you—gently, I hope—to take stock and to give up trying to be the center of the universe. That job is already taken, and the joy of that position already being filled is that we are able to fall into the hands of our Creator, rather than trying to take over His job. That is indeed a wondrous (yet reasonable) mystery; and mysteries are a part of life in which we stand in awe, compared to finding a problem, which is a puzzle to be solved.

I do not think that there are any original ideas in this book. I have relied heavily on much better authors than I. But what I hope this work may do is to encourage Christians to look at all aspects

---

[3] Greg Lukianoff and Jonathan Haidt, *The Coddling of the American Mind: How Good Intentions and Bad Ideas Are Setting Up a Generation For Failure* (Westminster: Penguin Books, 2018).

[4] J.P. Moreland, *Scientism and Secularism: Learning to Respond to a Dangerous Ideology* (Wheaton: Crossway, 2018).

of life through the lens of knowing Christ so that life can be seen more clearly. That includes how we think about our thinking.

Grace and peace,

Stephen J. Fyson, Ph.D.

Chapter 1
THINKING AND THE BIBLE

"THAT'S THE PASSAGE. HOW DOES each of us feel about it?" The Bible study leader waited caringly and patiently for responses.

"I feel that this is a really important verse for me at this time in my life," said one participant. "There is something deep inside me that tells me this is a verse for me right now."

"Thank you for sharing that important verse for you," said the leader. "Anyone else?" There was almost an awkward silence.

"Well," said another member, somewhat hesitantly, "I am not sure about what Anne just said."

Anne looked shocked, in a polite kind of way.

"You see, I think that this verse is a principle for anyone who calls himself a Christian. So, in a sense, yes, it is a verse for her; but it is a verse for all of us, all the time." Rashad looked down to the ground because he could see in some people's faces that they did not like what he said.

The leader said, "Rashad, thank you for your point; but we look to validate all the comments in the group, so we work very hard here to not be critical or to offer correctives of other members."

At this, Anne smiled with increased confidence at her friends in the group. Rashad noticed.

"I am sorry if I offended anyone." Rashad certainly sounded sincere. "But I thought we were here to share our ideas so that we could understand God's Word better—"

The leader cut him off. "Let's you and I have a chat about that afterward, Rashad. It's time for us to ask what others might feel about these verses tonight. Anyone else?"

Rashad sat quietly and politely while others shared about what verses felt important to them.

HOW DO WE KNOW?

You may or may not have been in a situation like the one in the story above. I have seen these kinds of interactions for over forty years. Sometimes, such tensions are responded to with grace, patience, and longsuffering. At other times, not so much. Sadly, and too often, these discussions are not resolved in the unity that God has called us to in Jesus Christ (John 17:20-23; Eph. 4:3). The purpose of this little book is to help respond to this kind of situation by understanding more clearly the answer to the question, "From where do our ideas come?"

The question is not with reference to what we read, who we listen to, and our own proclivities. No, it is more the question of, "How is it that we are able to have thoughts, ideas, desires, and preferences?" The hope is that in exploring these themes, we can come to understand more about *how* we think and then be able to have clearer discussions about *what* we think.

For example, did you notice in the story above that some in the group emphasized how they *felt*? The alternative idea was expressed as a principled thought. Does this matter? In our day and age, it does. This is not to suggest that we have to become legalistic in our language when we are having heart-level conversations about life and faith. But it does suggest that if we understood more clearly from where our ideas are coming, we may be able to better discuss and discern truth and grace in matters of doctrine and experience and reason and emotions.

Such a proposal also suggests that the relationship between emotions and principled thought does matter in our world. The reason for exploring this idea will be unpacked more later when we investigate the kind of thinking about thinking that seems to be dominant in our current Western societies. For now, and as too brief a summary, I will simply say that the pendulum has swung—in our Western world, at least—to an individualistic decision-making process based on a therapeutically attuned morality expressed via emotivist language, narratives, and tribal rivalries. The result of such decision-making is often an extreme expression of individualized, perceived liberty. As I noted, more on this later.

Given this context, what are we to do as Christians? Following in the footsteps of two classics of the late J. I. Packer, we are to study God's Word to take us on the journey of "knowing God," and of "knowing man," within the prayerfulness of the fellowship of believers and with the guidance of His Holy Spirit. But it is in the Word of God that we are anchored; for in that Word, we see revealed the One Who is both Savior and Lord. Anything else is ultimately, to paraphrase Packer, will-of-the-wisp thinking. For indeed, the most audacious claim about Christianity is that it is true. Thus, it makes sense that it is through the lens of Christ's life and ministry that Christians can understand reality more clearly.[5][6]

Sometimes, Christian authors build up to unpacking what the Bible says about their topic or theme. However, in this book, we will look to describe some important aspects from the Bible first and then see how this picture can help steer us through a number of key aspects about thinking.

THE BIBLE AND HUMAN THINKING

The question about how it is that we can think is not only considered by Christians. Indeed, philosophers of all kinds have written on this topic across millennia. It is to one such thinker that we will turn as an introduction to some biblical principles about thinking. That person is Dr. Thomas Nagel. In his book, *Mind and Cosmos*, Dr. Nagel admits that the current dominant theory, which he called "naturalism," cannot account for how we think. Naturalism, in this context, is the belief or "ungrounded assumption" that everything in our world is explained by understanding the physics and chemistry of matter.[7] Those who believe in naturalism do not

---

5 J. I. Packer, *Knowing God* (London: Hodder and Stoughton, 1973).
6 J. I. Packer, *Knowing Man* (Englewood: Cornerstone Books, 1979).
7 Thomas Nagel, *Mind and Cosmos: Why the Materialist Neo-Darwinian Conception of Nature Is Almost Certainly False* (Oxford: Oxford University Press, 2012), 12.

believe in the non-physical aspects of reality with which the Bible commences, "In the beginning, God . . . " (Gen. 1:1).

However, for transparent atheists like Nagel, rejection of the existence of a Mind bringing into being the design in the universe is unsatisfactory if an alternative is not proposed. While outlining the difficulties that naturalism has in explaining what we know to be true in how we as humans function, Nagel notes that "thought, reasoning, and evaluation . . . are the functions that have enabled us to transcend the perspective of the immediate life-world given to us by our sense and instincts."[8]

Nagel concedes that these *thought* functions are possible because "mind is not just an afterthought or an accident or an add-on, but a basic aspect of nature."[9] Contrary to Nagel's (best guess) of mentality being part of physical matter, the Bible gives us a much clearer description of the basics of nature, or what it terms "Creation." It is through that lens that we will briefly review core aspects of reality in our world of thinking.

OUR STARTING POINT IS GOD

The Bible does not start by arguing about God's existence. It assumes it. His revealed Word to us in Scripture does not make sense unless we can accept that God is real.

Genesis 1:1-2 says, "In the beginning, God created the heavens and the earth. The earth was without form and void, and darkness

---

8 Ibid, 71.
9 Ibid, 16.

was over the face of the deep. And the Spirit of God was hovering over the face of the waters."

Some other passages that highlight this truth are Psalm 19:1-6 and Romans 1:18-20. In Psalm 19, David declares that the majesty of the heavens give loud testimony to God. The apostle Paul notes the same in his letter to the Romans and adds that there are moral consequences if we ignore the reality of the Creator while using the gifts He has given to us.

Why does this matter in terms of thinking? Professor John Lennox from Oxford makes the point that based on these explanations in Scripture, reality is best described when spirituality is understood as primary to matter.[10] This is seen, for example when the apostle John noted, "'God is spirit, and those who worship him must worship in spirit and truth'" (John 4:24). Because the Creator God is Spirit, He was before any physical matter came to be. God spoke our good world into being (Gen. 1; John 1). Lennox explains the commencement process of our world as requiring "the immateriality of information."[11] Such information was needed for our planet to come into existence. Therefore, spiritual reality existed before our physical/spiritual world.

BEING MADE IN GOD'S IMAGE

Throughout chapter one of Genesis, we see God speaking into the mess that was our universe. His words made this planet

---

10 John Lennox, *2084: Artificial Intelligence and the Future of Humanity* (Grand Rapids: Zondervan Reflective, 2020), 125.
11 Ibid, 117.

good so that we can live in it and be His representatives. Our delegated work was to continue doing His good work, which is what "made in His image" means.

> Then God said, 'Let us make man in our image, after our likeness. And let them have dominion over the fish of the sea and over the birds of the heavens and over the livestock and over all the earth and over every creeping thing that creeps on the earth.' So God created man in his own image, in the image of God he created him; male and female he created them (Gen. 1:26-27).

In these Bible verses, we can see our purpose, or function, being presented as another foundation for understanding who we are. That is, male and female were made for the purpose of being God's representatives. This teaching provides a clear basis for explaining the human desire to know, understand, and see meaning and purpose in life. Thus, in the Bible, one starting assumption about thinking is that it is given to us for a purpose; and that purpose is to do the good work He has prepared for us in Christ (Eph. 2:10).

We are all made in His image, which brings a context of deep respect for all persons and their thinking because we are all made in the Creator's image. However, we are images only. This means we are not gods, so there also needs to be some humility within our thinking.[12]

---

[12] Christopher Watkin, *Thinking Through Creation: Genesis 1 and 2 as Tools of Cultural Critique.* (Phillipsburg: P and R Publishing, 2017), 90.

BEING MADE TO DO GOOD

As noted above, Genesis 1 helps us understand that we were made to continue God's good work. Is this simply part of our Creation account, or is it also linked to the Gospel of Jesus Christ? These next verses from the apostle Paul help us see the link between this starting assumption of Scripture and the unfolding revelation of who we are if we believe in Jesus:

> But God, being rich in mercy, because of the great love with which he loved us, even when we were dead in our trespasses, made us alive together with Christ—by grace you have been saved... For by grace you have been saved through faith. And this is not your own doing; it is the gift of God, not a result of works, so that no one may boast. For we are his workmanship, created in Christ Jesus for good works, which God prepared beforehand, that we should walk in them (Eph. 2:4-5, 8-10).

God is Love; and the offer to be reconciled to Him, despite our sin, is given in grace. That is why Jesus Christ died for all people. The opportunity we have before God is to "'believe in him whom he has sent,'" as Jesus explained in John 6:29. It is through these gifts ("charismata") given to us to use for good that we can extend the good of God's grace ("charis") if we believe in Jesus. The apostle Peter explained it this way: "As each has received a gift, use it to serve one another, as good stewards of God's varied grace: whoever speaks, as one who speaks oracles of God; whoever serves, as one who serves by the strength that God supplies—in order that in everything God may be glorified through Jesus Christ. To him belong glory and dominion forever and ever. Amen" (1 Peter 4:10-11).

These frames of reference are foundational when we come to considering the mode of our thinking and the fruit of our thinking, to which we are called as human beings. The Message expresses these ideas this way: "No, we neither make nor save ourselves. God does both the making and saving. He creates each of us by Christ Jesus to join him in the work he does, the good work he has gotten ready for us to do, work we had better be doing" (Eph. 2:8-10).

OUR REFERENCE POINT IS SCRIPTURE

As you will have noted already, the reference point I am using to understand God, with reference to implications for thinking, is the Bible. Here is one example of why this is important:

> See, I have taught you statutes and rules, as the Lord my God commanded me, that you should do them in the land that you are entering to take possession of it. Keep them and do them, for that will be your wisdom and your understanding in the sight of the peoples, who, when they hear all these statutes, will say, "Surely this great nation is a wise and understanding people." For what great nation is there that has a god so near to it as the Lord our God is to us, whenever we call upon him? And what great nation is there, that has statutes and rules so righteous as all this law that I set before you today? (Deut. 4:5-8).

14   Why Good Thinking Starts with God

This Bible passage explains that God revealed His will to us so that we would know how to live. Such knowledge brought understanding and wisdom. This is the product of right thinking. However, knowing how to live—and, thus, the way to think—was done much more openly before the Fall in Genesis 3:

> The Woman said to the serpent, "Not at all. We can eat from the trees in the garden. It's only about the tree in the middle of the garden that God said, 'Don't eat from it; don't even touch it or you'll die.'" The serpent told the Woman, "You won't die. God knows that the moment you eat from that tree, you'll see what's really going on. You'll be just like God, knowing everything, ranging all the way from good to evil." When the Woman saw that the tree looked like good eating and realized what she would get out of it—she'd know everything!—she took and ate the fruit and then gave some to her husband, and he ate (Gen. 3:2-6, The Message).

We see in this part of the account of our beginnings that we humans decided to make up our own minds about what is right and wrong. This had a radical impact on our thinking processes.

The verses from Deuteronomy 4 explain that God's expectation was for His "called people" to live as He made us to live. As just noted, when that happens, others outside the community will want to know why they are so wise—that is, when we live according to how our Creator made us to live, others can see wisdom in our thinking and can then be curious about that. Jesus expressed the same idea when He taught, "'You are the light of the world. A city set on a hill cannot be hidden. Nor do people light a lamp and put it under a basket, but on a stand, and it gives light to all in the house. In the same way, let your light shine before others, so that they may see your good works and give glory to your Father who is in heaven'" (Matt. 5:14-16).

This is the vision for mature community as expressed in Scripture. But it is only through Scripture that we know what this life together looks like with the help of God's Holy Spirit guiding us. As the apostle Paul wrote, "Until I come, devote yourself to the public reading of Scripture, to exhortation, to teaching" (1 Tim. 4:13). And in 2 Timothy 3:16-17, he explains further the reason why we should devote ourselves to Scripture: "All Scripture is breathed out by God and profitable for teaching, for reproof, for correction, and for training in righteousness, that the man of God may be complete, equipped for every good work."

From briefly reviewing some of the starting assumptions in the Bible, we can see that we are called to live as our Creator intended. That means knowing the Scriptures. This is more than knowing about what the Bible teaches us. It means that we are to be committed to what it teaches. We do not go to the Bible to prove our point of view. We go to the Bible to be renewed in our thinking and, therefore, transformed in our living (Rom. 12:1-2).

THINKING AND MIND IN THE BIBLE

We will now turn to some of the more specific principles about thinking as revealed in the Bible. A point to note as we commence this short review is that this process of understanding the meaning of thinking in the Bible can involve more than considering the words "thought" and "thinking." A very useful booklet that explains this systematically is called *The Bible and the Human Mind* by J.C. Metcalfe.[13]

The principles from the Bible that we have identified thus far point us in the direction to understand why thinking is such an important part of life, and that is because it is part of us being made in the image of God to do His good work. Scripture also describes that our relationships with God and each other are broken because of self-focused thinking—that is, we like to morally decide what is right and wrong without taking notice of our Creator's intentions. We have also noted that these thinking processes reflect that understanding reality includes accepting spiritual aspects of life.

Another implication is that our purpose of doing God's good work points us to understand why good thinking needs to start with God. Without accepting His reality (and that He is Spirit), our understanding of everything becomes "futile" or "meaningless" or "darkened"—to use the language of Ephesians 4:17-19 and Romans 1. We see this pattern consistently in passages in the Bible, where thinking relates to using our minds for reasoning and, having reasoned, to make choices that inform our commitments. Some of the key words from the Bible that help clarify these aspects of our human reality will now be described.

---

13   J. C. Metcalfe, *The Bible and the Human Mind* (Fort Worth: CLC Publications, 1996).

SOME KEY WORDS AND THEIR IMPORTANCE

Below are the key words from the Bible that give us guidance in understanding the nature of thinking for us as human beings made in the image of God.

THE MIND ("NOUS")

We could have started this exploration by asking the question, "What is the relationship between mind and thinking?" We will indeed progressively unpack this dynamic relationship, and our starting point in this journey continues to be the Bible. We will summarize its use of "mind" and "thoughts" in these first two introductory descriptions.

Metcalfe explains that the focus of "nous" in the New Testament indicates "reflective consciousness."[14] He observes this through the writing of the apostle Paul in particular. Metcalfe notes that this meaning of the mind is distinct from responses that derive from impulses ("without thought"). As such, the use of "mind" involves taking "cognisance of external objects and denotes the reasoning faculty."[15]

For the apostle Paul, this capacity of our minds—to reason about reality—is central to understanding core processes in human relationships. His use of mind in Romans 1 makes it clear that human rejection of God, despite His desire for us to be in reconciled relationship with Him (vs. 18-33), results in a "debased

---
14   Metcalfe, 6.
15   Ibid.

mind" (v. 28). Such depravity is evidenced in how we live in the intimate and public spheres of our lives. Rejection of God in thinking and in subsequent ways of living results in increased sensuality and sexual rebellion (or, technically expressed, perversion) and also in heartlessness.

Paul summarizes this process succinctly and dramatically in Ephesians 4:17-24. Paul contrasts "futile thinking" (v. 17) with being "renewed in the spirit of your minds" (v. 23). The analysis that is given in this passage, like that in Romans, is not some abstract philosophical opinion to prove some ephemeral point. No, Paul goes on to explain that futile thinking, which comes from a heart that denies the reality of God in our lives, has drastic implications for how we live. He reveals that when our thinking ignores God, it leads to insensitivity ("beyond feeling") and then to increased "sensuality, greedy to practice every kind of impurity" (v. 19).

The contrast of this decline into addictive patterns of life is "to put on a new self," which is committed, with God's help, to live the way we were created to live (v. 24). These warnings and patterns are repeated for different contexts in Colossians 2:18, 2 Thessalonians 2:2, and 1 Timothy 6:3-5. The Christians in these circumstances are being clearly taught that there is spiritual work to be discerned so that their minds can reason correctly. "Correct reasoning" in this context means that they can understand God's reality in that moment with the help of God's Holy Spirit. To not avail themselves of this gift of grace is to lend themselves to unsettled, corrupt, and relationally dysfunctional ways of life.

Importantly, and consistent with one of our themes so far (that good thinking starts with God), the Bible teaches that our faculty for good and proper reasoning reflects God's character. For example, we see in Romans 11:34 that Paul asks (in quoting Isaiah 40:13), "'For who has known the mind of the Lord?'" The same word "nous" is used in this context. This helps us understand that thinking with our minds can reflect God's proactive thought and action, as this is also highlighted in the use of "nous" in passages such as 1 Corinthians 14, where Paul insists that what happens in our congregational meetings needs to involve our minds, or "understanding," and not just be governed by mindless impulses, even spiritual impulses that bypass our thinking.

Human thinking that reflects spiritual reality is also reflected in passages such as Titus 1:15, which describes the morally aesthetic directions of our minds. Are they toward God's purity (holiness and righteousness) or not? Similarly, in Luke 24:45, we see that Jesus had to "open their minds" so that the disciples could make sense of the realities described in Scripture. The block in the disciples' thinking was not lack of knowing *about* the passages in Scripture. It was their spiritual slowness of heart that impacted their minds. Relieving such spiritual blocks to thinking is, in the language of Poplin, real spiritual business; and it is not properly described by using reductionist psycho-social neurological language.[16]

---

[16] Barry Kanpol and Mary Poplin, eds.,"Blinded by Secular Interpretations of Religious Knowledge," in *Christianity and the Secular Border Control: The Loss of Judeo-Christian Knowledge* (Critical Education and Ethics) (Bern: Peter Lang, Inc., International Academic Publishers, 2017).

Revelation 13:18 and 17:9 demonstrates that such a spiritual transaction between God's Holy Spirit and our minds leads to wisdom—that is, the ability to see reality clearly and to act accordingly. Thus, we can see already in this consideration of "nous" that the Bible does not allow for a center of intentional thought that is neutral when it comes to thinking—for our minds draw us closer to God's reality, or not, as an outworking of the state of our hearts.

THOUGHTS ("NOEMA")

It is one thing to have a mind, but how do we know what it does? It is through our thoughts. Metcalfe describes thoughts as "the product of the action of "nous,"" or that thought is the expression of our mind, and notes that "noema" only occurs six times in the New Testament, four of those being in 2 Corinthians.

In 2 Corinthians 3 and 4, we see the same pattern as explained by Paul about the mind—if hearts are hard toward God, then our thoughts cannot make sense. Such petrification against God's Holy Spirit means that good thoughts stay in the shadows when trying to understand reality. The same theme occurs again in 2 Corinthians 10:3-5. The contrast is stark. We can, in our thinking, stay captive to ideas about life that exclude the reality of God; or we can regain clarity and responsiveness by seeing Jesus for Who He is. In chapter eleven verse three, Paul extends his concern to hoping the Corinthians would not be led astray from their belief in Christ and that their clear-mindedness would keep them with "sincere and pure devotion to Christ."

Such a way of thinking needs help. That help comes from the Spirit of Christ, which brings to life the hoped for "shalom" to which God's people are called. In Philippians 4:7, Paul clarifies that it is such peace that "will guard your hearts and minds through Christ Jesus."

We therefore see again a pattern which does not allow a non-spiritual approach to our thinking; and because of that, we are also not allowed to suggest thinking about life and reality as neutral. That is, our thinking points toward things unseen but eternal; or it pretends such spiritual realities are not needed in our moral, ethical, and relational decision-making. For example, when we are considering a moral issue such as how much alcohol to drink, do we consider that the Creator God Who made us is interested in our thoughts about this or just go by what our friends and feelings are telling us? Do we believe in the "eternal perspective" that Paul teaches in Ephesians 5:18: "And do not get drunk with wine, for that is debauchery, but be filled with the Spirit"? Or do we say to ourselves, "That is not important for now and eternity, so maybe I will look at that if things get too bad with my drinking"? How we respond to situations such as this reflect whether our thinking is toward eternity or not.

REASONING ("DIALOGISMOS")

If we have a mind that enables thoughts, the Bible also notes in various ways that we are able to reason about life in general and to consider the contexts in which we find ourselves. There are numerous New Testament examples of such "diagolismos" being part of what unfolds, and we will review just a few.

The first reference in both Matthew 15:19 and Mark 7:21 highlights one of the propositions of this book—that our thinking is a reflection of who we are as human beings made in the image of God. Our thoughts are not simply a matter of our genetic inheritance and capacity (what some call our "natures'"); nor is our thinking just an outcome of our social context past and present (what some would call our "nurture"). These are both important, but Jesus clearly teaches that it is the heart—our innermost selves, the center of our embodied soulness—that is the seat of our life-thinking, of our thoughts about meaning, purpose, and right and wrong. For "what comes out of the mouth proceeds from the heart" (Matt. 15:18).

As noted earlier, this is a spiritual reality. That is why Christians speak of discernment or, as the young King Solomon described it, understanding what is right and wrong before God in our spirits (2 Kings 3). Examples of this reality in action can be seen in other places where this word is used in the New Testament. In Luke 9:46-49, we read of Jesus "knowing the reasoning of their hearts" when the disciples were disputing about greatness. Earlier in Luke we read of Jesus doing the same with others—some doubted His capacity to forgive sins; and in perceiving their thoughts, Jesus heals a paralytic (Luke 5:17-26). In Luke 6:6-11, He also knows their thoughts (how they were reasoning) about healing on the Sabbath and He again gives an object lesson about the true spirit of the truth by restoring a withered hand. In each case, Jesus is discerning the inaccurate reasoning and responding with a question and action that gets to the real spirit of the matter.

Such discernment by Jesus was also sometimes cause for comfort, as demonstrated in Luke 24:36-40 when Jesus reassured the disciples that He had indeed risen from the dead. Such enactment of this perfect discernment is explained by Paul in 1 Corinthians 3:20, where Psalm 94:11 is invoked to remind the Corinthians that the Lord knows our reasoning thoughts perfectly. We see the same spiritual exchange noted in the generic context of Romans 1:21, where God discerns the futility of thinking from people who wish to push Him aside while enjoying His gifts to them. The results of such flawed ("hard-hearted") reasoning are not good.

Paul calls this "not good reasoning" as "lofty opinion raised against the knowledge of God" (1 Cor. 10:5), which is the opposite of starting with God in our thinking. We cannot change our thinking against the knowledge of God by ourselves—we need the Spirit of Christ to help us "renew our minds" (Rom. 12:2) so that we can become "new creations" (Gal. 6:15), where the only thing that counts is "faith working through love" (Gal. 5:6).

PATTERNS OF UNDERSTANDING ("DIANOIA")

If we have a mind that enables thoughts which are the structure of our reasoning—then we can also observe patterns in our thinking, or understanding. This Greek word can sometimes also be translated "mind"; but in its infrequent use in the New Testament, it seems to relate to our patterned ways of thinking that have consequences.

We can see this in one of our previous key passages in Ephesians 4:18, where the pattern of ignoring God in our thinking is outlined, as it is in Colossians 1:21. Paul explains that it is a focus on ungodly desires that is the corrupting pattern of thinking in these minds (Eph. 2:1-3). The contrasting pattern of thinking is presented in the prayer of Ephesians 1:18, where it is an openness of the heart toward God that is the crux of understanding and hope. This pattern of a movement toward deepening relationship with God that includes our thinking (understanding reality as God does) is also presented in Hebrews where Old Testament promises from God about His coming actions are remembered (Heb. 8:10-11, 10:16). Peter confirms that this process assumes a proactive desire and reception on our part (1 Peter 1:13).

THE HEART ("KARDIA")

We have previously noted that "heart" is our spiritual center from which our thoughts come (e.g., Eph. 4:18; Luke 6:45). A classic way of expressing this aspect of reality is that the human heart (not the physical one) is the seat of who we are with reference to our desires, affections, thoughts, and will. It is, therefore, the platform from where we can choose to express our human dignity and morality. The heart is the basis of human dignity because it represents God's Spirit being breathed into our personhood as described in Genesis 1:26-27. The heart is also the basis of morality because it is God's breath within us that enables transcendence of thought (thinking that can evaluate instinctual responses) so that we can decide how to respond to our physical selves and our social selves (what we earlier called the "nature" and "nurture" aspects of life).

Metcalfe uses the metaphor of the heart being like the roots of a tree—from it comes either nutrition or death. It is why we saw the apostle Paul regularly challenge his readers to consider whether their hearts were hard or soft toward God and to consider the consequences for their lives. A passage that expounds such principles clearly is Romans 10:8-10: "But what does it say? 'The word is near you, in your mouth and in your heart' (that is, the word of faith that we proclaim); because, if you confess with your mouth that Jesus is Lord and believe in your heart that God raised him from the dead, you will be saved. For with the heart one believes and is justified, and with the mouth one confesses and is saved."

Thankfully, God also reassures us that we do not have to carry cares in our hearts because He knows our hearts and cares for us in ways that we cannot know, since He knows us better than we know ourselves (1 John 3:18-22). This is important because we are also told that we can allow our hearts to be deceived (Jer. 17:9; James 1:26). In contrast again, and as a cause for joy for those who confess Jesus as Lord, our hearts can be "cleansed by faith in Christ, [and] becomes His dwelling place by His Spirit (Eph. 3:17)."[17]

This spiritual dynamic of life, with reference to thinking about thinking, is why the laments and praises that we see in the Psalms have remained fresh to millions of people across millennia. Perhaps one of the most quoted psalms in private and public times that captures

---

17   Metcalfe, 78.

the reality of our hearts is Psalm 51, which includes these verses that beautifully convey some of these spiritual aspects of our reality:

> Have mercy on me, O God, according to your steadfast love; according to your abundant mercy blot out my transgressions. Wash me thoroughly from my iniquity, and cleanse me from my sin . . . Create in me a clean heart, O God, and renew a right spirit within me. Cast me not away from your presence, and take not your Holy Spirit from me. Restore to me the joy of your salvation, and uphold me with a willing spirit . . . For you will not delight in sacrifice, or I would give it; you will not be pleased with a burnt offering. The sacrifices of God are a broken spirit; a broken and contrite heart, O God, you will not despise.

A BRIEF MENTION OF SOME OTHER RELATED WORDS

UNDERSTANDING ("GNOSIS")

This word and its derivatives appear almost thirty times in the New Testament and can be regarded as receiving and comprehending true information. It is the basis of "knowing about" life. In that sense, such knowledge can be based on truth or a lie. It can also be responded to very differently. For example, everyone who passes a driving test has demonstrated correct knowledge or understanding of the road rules. That does not mean they will necessarily obey the road rules when they drive. Thus, the New Testament speaks of those with understanding (knowledge) but who respond in dangerous ways (e.g., Luke 11:52). Paul will sometimes celebrate the understanding that people have of the Gospel, but he will also chastise them when they do not live accordingly (e.g., Rom. 2:17-23; 1 Cor. 8:1-3). Paul's warning about using information to "puff ourselves up" may be why Peter taught that if understanding is to be used well, we should add other virtues to it—self-control, perseverance, godliness, brotherly kindness, and charity (love) (2 Peter 1:5-7).

PRACTICAL WISDOM ("SOPHIA")

The traditional (Old Testament) usage extended to the New Testament is seen in Luke 2:40, where it notes that Jesus grows in wisdom. This indicates knowledge of God's ways (through His laws, decrees, and precepts, according to Psalm 119) which translates into God-honoring words and actions. Sometimes, Jesus is described as wisdom personified (e.g., 1 Cor. 1:30; Col. 2:2-3) because He came in grace and truth (John 1:14, 17). That is why growth in Christian knowledge can be called wisdom (Eph. 1:8; Col. 1:9). So, it seems that when our minds produce thoughts that lead to good reasoning and understanding of reality because we are responding to God's mercy, the result is wisdom as God defines it.

SOME KEY IMPLICATIONS FOR THINKING ABOUT THINKING

Our exploration of biblical principles related to our God-given purpose in life, together with key words in Scripture, has highlighted why thinking (using our minds) carries spiritual importance. That is, thinking—good thinking—needs to start with God. In summary, here are some examples from Scripture that unpack these truths as we close this chapter:

- We are either enemies in our minds toward God (Col. 1:21), or we are "tak[ing] every thought captive to obey Christ" (2 Cor. 10:3-5).
- Our thinking is darkened and futile when we push God away (Rom. 1:16-32; Eph. 4:17-19).
- Instead, we are asked to not conform to the patterns of this world but to be renewing our minds in response to God's mercy (Rom. 12:1-2; Eph. 4:20-24).
- It is why our thinking can be driven by our flesh (instincts) or by the Holy Spirit (Rom. 8:5-11; Col. 2:18; 1 Peter 2:12, 17-19; Jude 10).

These Bible passages make it clear that thinking is not neutral. They explain that our thinking is either drawing us closer to God by helping us more clearly understand Who He is as a response to His mercy, or it is not. We may be clever, but that is not the same as being wise (1 Cor. 1:18-31). Good thinking, therefore, starts with our relationship with God.

A NOTE ABOUT EPHESIANS 4:23 AND PHILIPPIANS 2:5

One of the themes of this chapter is that the Bible proclaims that spirituality is real, primary, and linked (foundationally) to understanding our thinking. However, we live in a therapeutically moral age, where our reasoning can be called "emotivist." Such a dominance of psychologized structures of thought (which often diminish or negate spiritual aspects of reality) can have an impact on our thinking about thinking, and that, sometimes, can even have an impact on how we understand words in the Bible.

These verses exemplify this temptation in translation. Some versions used the word "attitude" for a while, before changing to alternatives such as "mindset" or just "mind." This last version is closest to the original because, as we have seen, the "mind" in the Bible infers spirituality being part of the thinking process. Because human beings are souls in a body, how we think (beyond instinct) is not based on some aspect of life outside of our relationship with God. That is the inference when we use phrases like, "It is just my personality that drives my attitude."

Gordon Fee summarized this problem well when he suggested that in evangelical thinking, we describe ourselves as trinitarians but can think too often (and then act) as binitarians—that is, we too often ignore the role of the Holy Spirit in our everyday lives as Christians. He traced the history of how the Christian Church misused the adjective "spiritual" with reference to biblical texts and undertook an exegesis of 1 Corinthians 2:14-15 as an example of this. Fee noted that such an exploration is not simply a theoretical enterprise. If we say we are trinitarian but live as binitarians, then:

> In their practical life in the world, there is very little self-conscious awareness of ones' life being filled with, or led by, the Holy Spirit . . . it is obvious that if

the Holy Spirit is left out of our account of Christian spirituality, then a very great deal will have been lost. Spirituality without the Holy Spirit is a feeble human project . . . there is scarcely an aspect of genuinely Christian life that is not "spiritual" in the Pauline sense, of being lived in and by means of the so-called third person of the Trinity.[18]

Let us call on the Holy Spirit's guidance as we continue our journey of thinking about thinking.

---

18 Gordon Fee, "Getting the Spirit Back into Spirituality," in *Life in the Spirit: Spiritual Formation in Theological Perspective* (Wheaton Theology Conference Series), Jeffrey Greenman and George Kalantzis, eds. (Downers Grove: IVP Academic, 2010), 37, 42.

Chapter 2
THINKING AND CONSCIOUSNESS

TWO YOUNG FRIENDS WERE SITTING on a grassy hill overlooking the water and were ruminating out loud together. One said in a dreamy way, "Have you ever wanted to just be a bird?"

"Why?" shot back the friend, in a less-than-dreamy way. "And are you talking about those seagulls down there or the eagles up there?"

The birds were in view of both friends, who wondered at their capacities of care-free flight.

"I don't mind because both of them just do what they do without caring about tomorrow, or next year, or, well, without any of that stuff that we worry and sweat over."

"Well, yes, you are right about them not worrying," said the good friend, now sitting up and facing her life-long buddy. "But they miss out on a lot, which I do not care to give up!"

The emphasis at the end of this comment caused the first friend to be more alert, and he faced his mate as he asked, "What are you talking about? What could be better than simply eating, flying, making babies, and not worrying? Miss out on what?"

"Hmmm... well, the kinds of things I had in mind were, you know, falling in love, having dreams together, setting up a home, and being part of a community of people who care."

In a voice almost a whisper, he simply said, "Oh, of course..." As his voice trailed off on the outside, inwardly, he was screaming at himself, "Oops! "You dolt!" This was the second time he had not picked up on his "best mate's" emotions. You see, his best mate was the woman he was hoping to ask to be his wife.

WHAT IS A GOOD THEORY?

Have you ever been part of a conversation like the one in the story above (perhaps without the romantic overtones)? Maybe the conversation has only been in your own head. Can you see why the young dreamer had not reflected on the realities that we described in chapter one—that human beings are spiritual in a way that animals are not? Both have consciousness, but only human beings have self-consciousness. Humans are made in the image of God, and He has made us as embodied souls. Animals are not created in the same way. This fact may be upsetting for some people, but let us see why this makes sense with reference to the Bible and our experiences.

In the previous chapter, we saw that the Bible teaches us that our mind, thoughts, and reasoning have a spiritual direction. But how do we know this personally? Such questions can tempt us to become very introverted if we dwell on them too much. Indeed, this line of thinking can be similar to theologians debating how many angels can fit onto the head of a pin! Yet in this book, we want to continue to reflect on what our thoughts are, from where they originate, and what we can do with them.

However, remember why ideas are important to understand. As beings who think, we test things out in more than practical ways. We search for truth. Truth-seeking is closely linked to our sense of justice and injustice. We look for ways to make sense of what is right, wrong, good, bad, beautiful, and ugly. When undertaking these mental pursuits, thinking about thinking will only be helpful if we believe the ideas we examine are based on good theories and descriptions. How do we know what a good theory is? Borrowing from authors like Dallas Willard and Mary Poplin, this book will assume that a good theory helps explain reality better.

If this is true, then how do we know what reality is? As a Christian, I believe that the Creator of the universe (the God of the Christian Bible) has provided enough information (and experiences) to testify to what is real based on His character and actions. Others have noted that when we believe in Jesus Christ, we not only understand what He has done for us and but also learn why we see everything else in life more clearly.

One of those people is Gregory Koukl, who summarizes the focus of the story of the Bible by considering the question, "What is Christianity?" Koukl responds, "Christianity is first and foremost a picture of reality, a view of the way the world is."[19]

---

19 Gregory Koukl, *The Story of Reality: How the World Began, How It Ends, and Everything Important That Happens in Between* (Grand Rapids: Zondervan, 2017), 27.

Mary Poplin, a tenured professor of education, experienced the impact of understanding reality as a Christian this way: "When I first began to explore Christianity I had in mind that it would be simply about my personal life, mostly my emotions. It might help me be a better person. Little did I realize it was more rational, all encompassing [sic] and intellectually demanding than any secular philosophy, or scientific, social or psychological theory I had or could ever encounter."[20]

This is what Christopher Watkin helpfully described as looking at life through a "Biblical Critical Theory." He noted that people's overarching theories, often called worldviews, are not simply ways of thinking about life; but they are like a critical lens through which we make sense of everything else. This is similar to Poplin's term for these basic assumptions: "operating systems of the mind"[21] [22] Some commonly held worldview theories are feminist theory, cultural neo-Marxist theory, capitalist theory, or intersectionality theory.

How might such starting points make a difference when thinking about thinking? Here are some examples from Watkin who uses his Biblical Critical Theory to explore questions, such as "Are people basically good or bad?" and "How do we know if our knowledge is right?" In response to the first question, some would suggest that people are born good, but our imperfect society messes

---

20 Mary Poplin, *Is Reality Secular?: Testing the Assumptions of Four Global Worldviews* (Westmont: InterVarsity Press, 2014), 211.
21 Ibid.
22 Watkin, ibid.

them up. In response to the second, others might say that true knowledge only comes from the scientific method, and everything else is spurious. In contrast to these assumptions, Watkin references the biblical teaching from Genesis 1:26 that records the start of the human race as follows: "Then God said, 'Let us make man' in our image, after our likeness. And let them have dominion over the fish of the sea and over the birds of the heavens and over the livestock and over all the earth and over every creeping thing that creeps on the earth.'"

Consistent with what we noted in chapter one, Watkin highlights that we can understand that we are not gods (we are only in God's image). This protects us from being too proud about who we are. But because our image is "of God," we "are not nothing."[23] This is in contrast to atheists, who say that we best understand ourselves as physical matter that moves through time, guided only by chance.

Similarly, and with reference to the second question about the certainty of our knowledge, Watkin extends this part of Biblical Critical Theory to note, "We are created in God's *image*, and therefore our knowledge cannot be exhaustive; we are created in *God's* image, and therefore our knowledge is true."[24] This is again in contrast to those who do not admit that there are sources of

---

23 Cornelius Van Til, *Introduction to Systematic Theology*, William Edgar, ed. (Phillipsburg: P and R Publishing, 2007), 61, quoted in Christopher Watkin, Thinking Through Creation: Genesis 1 and 2 as Tools of Cultural Critique (Phillipsburg: P and R Publishing, 2017), 90.
24 Ibid, 91.

knowledge outside of the scientific method. Do these differences matter when thinking about thinking?

Dallas Willard describes what is at risk as "when desire conflicts with reality, sooner or later reality wins . . . Idolatry is a mistake about reality, and an error at the 'worldview' level."[25]

That is, when ideas are promoted because it is said they are describing reality but are not, they lead us into idolatry because they take us away from seeing the world as God's—the world that reflects His character. To misread the world is to misread God. Willard further explains this when he notes:

> In their effort to be in control of knowledge, they have redefined knowledge, through "specialization" and "professionalization," in such a way that it cannot deal with those questions. So real life, which must assume answers—is, as a matter of fact, abandoned by our "knowledge institutions" to feeling, force, politics and "traditions." Ragtag, incoherent "answers" float here and there, with no responsible clarification and critique.[26]

In this book, what is real about our thinking will be tested against the Word of God. We have laid the foundations for this by outlining the key words in the Bible that relate to thinking. Let us now use that platform to test the reality about the importance of our consciousness with relation to our thinking.

---

25 Dallas Willard, *Knowing Christ Today: Why We Can Trust Spiritual Knowledge* (San Francisco: Harper One, 2009, 41).
26 Ibid, 57.

WHAT ABOUT THINKING AND CONSCIOUSNESS?

Let us take another step back and ask if there is a helpful summary response to the question, "What is thinking?" *The International Webster New Encycopledic Dictionary* describes *thinking* as, "To form or conceive mentally, as a thought; to create intellectually, as an idea or concept; to speculate upon, meditate, or ponder."[27] This kind of description gives us an idea of the outcome of thinking but not what it really is. The dictionary explains what can happen when thinking takes place, but it is not very helpful in explaining from where our thoughts come and why.

Another approach to clarifying the nature of human thinking is to compare it with animal thinking. Biblically, we can note that the kind of thinking that humans do is distinctive when compared to animals (Gen. 1:24-27). The Spirit of God breathed into mankind (male and female) provides a self-consciousness that enables decision-making beyond instinct. This is why Augustine described the mind as "not in body as in a subject, as colour is in body, because the mind is a substance ... mind is not the organization of the body, but the mind is life."[28]

Augustine's use of "substance" is from the Greek language, and it indicates the essence that describes an entity (and not its physical

---

27 *The International Webster New Encyclopedic Dictionary of the English Language and Library of Useful Knowledge*, s.v. "thinking" (London: Tabor House, 1972), 1023.
28 *Aurelius Augustine, On Christian Teaching*, R. P. H. Green, trans. (Oxford: Oxford University Press, 2008), 76.

structure). Other philosophers use the contrasting language of "form" and "shape." The former conveys what an entity is in its functional totality, while the latter conveys the elements that make up the entity's presence. Ric Machuga explains it this way: "All things are composed of both form and shape. 'Form' is that which makes something what it is. 'Shape,' as we are using this term, refers to the totality of a thing's physically quantifiable properties, i.e. its physical shape, size, height, weight, chemical composition, etc., *in its most complete description.*"[29]

For example, a child asks, "What is this?" pointing to that on which we are sitting. If we answer in terms of form or substance, we will say, "This is a chair." If we answer in terms of, "This is a tree trunk that has been cut and shaped and joined together with glue and nails so that we can sit on it," we are answering (laboriously!) in terms of the shape and structure of the thing. Our capacity to think in both ways is a consequence of our self-consciousness.

Again, it is this self-consciousness in our thinking that enables us to choose differently to animals. The Eastern Orthodox Christian philosopher David Bentley Hart has reflected on this and compares a theistic understanding of consciousness with those who believe that all aspects of life are only material (physical matter). Such theorists consider that anything that we call consciousness leading to thinking must be reducible to

---

[29] Ric Machuga, *In Defense of the Soul: What It Means to Be Human* (Michigan: Brazos Press, 2002), 27.

"the interaction between our neurological constitution and the concrete world around us."[30]

Hart settles upon the concept of "embodied soulness" to explain that our thoughts come from a unified experience arising from "two conjoined but ontologically distinct kinds of substance."[31] Such embodied soulness is the platform which enables thought that is self-conscious. Gregory Koukl, in his explanation of the relevance of the Bible to these kinds of life issues, also explores the difference between animals and humans and reminds his readers that all sentient creatures have souls. But that does not make human beings, in their thinking, mere animals. As Koukl notes, "No, it is not having souls that distinguishes humans from animals. What makes us special is the kind of souls we have . . . When man is reduced to a mere animal . . . morality and human rights die and power is all that remains . . . Animals do what comes naturally. Humans should not."[32]

The choice that we have to check our instincts before acting is more than the limited choice of animals. It is a deeply moral capacity because we can think about what we are thinking about—that is, we not only have consciousness but also self-consciousness. As we saw from the "honest atheist" Thomas Nagel, this capacity for transcendence beyond "the immediate life-world given to us

---

30   David Bentley Hart, The Experience of God: Being, Consciousness, Bliss (New Haven and London: Yale University Press, 2013), 153.
31   Ibid, 156.
32   Koukl, 68, 71.

by our sense and instincts"[33] needs an explanation beyond "materialism," to use Koukl's term.

BUT WE DO HAVE DIFFERENT KINDS OF THINKING

Richard Swinburne helpfully described the difference between our *automatic* thinking and our more carefully *considered* thinking. He clarified what he believed was the dynamic relationship between brain and mind and outlined that sometimes the brain initiates behavior. The autonomic response of flight in the face of physical danger is an example. However, he also demonstrated that mental activity initiates physical activity, and this working of the mind ("in particular intentions") was non-physical. Swinburne considered autonomic-derived actions as "non-intentional causation" and mentally derived action as "intentional causation." For example, when our hand touches a surface that is harmfully hot, we automatically pull our hand away. This is non-intentional causation, but it is helpful in these kinds of instances.[34]

When we are considering whether to stop and help a person struggling next to us as they try to step onto a bus, that is an example of intentional causation. This latter example, and the myriad of examples like it in everyday life, are instances of us exercising our moral agency, based on self-consciousness, related to the spiritual aspect of our embodied soulness.

---

33 Nagel, ibid.
34 Richard Swinburne, *Mind, Brain, and Free Will* (Oxford: Oxford University Press, 2013).

Anthony O'Hear has also helped explain the importance of understanding such *self*-consciousness when reflecting on our thinking as humans. He delineates self-consciousness from consciousness because it enables not just response to the physical aspects of life, as received through our five senses. Self-consciousness enables the perceiver (us, in our thinking) to know we are the perceiver who is receiving our thoughts, and we can, therefore, have a remembered past and a conjectured future, all of which makes us "an agent in the world."[35]

What is also interesting in terms of implications for our thinking is that O'Hear explains the communal nature of our self-consciousness. He describes the relational aspects of self-conscious thinking as necessary for us to understand the reality of self because we can learn and interact through language with another. Put another way, without others, how could we determine who we are as a distinct, thinking being?

The theologian Walter Brueggemann suggested that to biblically answer the question "Who am I," we need to answer the question, "Whose am I?"[36] For Christians, that takes us to what the apostle John taught in his letters—that we must consider love of God and of others as integrally linked (1 John 2:9-11). This, in turn, reflects Jesus' answer to the supposedly tricky question about the most important commandment. Jesus noted that God's ways mean

---

35 Anthony O'Hear, *Beyond Evolution: Human Nature and the Limits of Evolutionary Explanation* (Oxford: Clarendon Press, 1997).
36 Walter Brueggemann, "Covenanting as Human Vocation: A Discussion of the Relation of the Bible and Pastoral Care," *Interpretation* 33, no. 2 (1979):115-29.

that we are to grow in love of God and love of others. These are the most crucial commandments to understand the Creator's intention for how we are to live as humans.

O'Hear applies his philosophical framework to come to a related point about life, thinking, and choices. If we are made to live in community, then we are not only agents that distinguish ourselves from others; but we are also moral agents. By virtue of our existence as self-conscious agents, we have some imperative both to admit the validity of the distinction and, in matters of belief, to seek the true rather than the merely useful and, in matters of desire, to seek the good rather than the merely useful.[37]

Or, as Christian Smith summarized it, "Humans are moral animals, rather, because they experience, in part as a result of their self-consciousness, a particular relationship to themselves and the world that evokes a search for standards beyond themselves by which they may evaluate themselves.[38]

That is, as self-conscious beings in relationship with other self-conscious beings, we seek that which is true and good. Animals (nor robots) do not do that. Our self-consciousness explains why we are meaning-seekers, and animals (nor robots) are not. It is also why we can worry in inordinate ways and worry ourselves into addictions, such as vengeance, greed, and a host of other relational dysfunctions that the apostle Paul called works of "the flesh" (Gal. 5:16-18).

---

37 Ibid.
38 Christian Smith, *Moral, Believing Animals: Human Personhood and Culture* (Oxford: Oxford University Press, 2009), 43.

Like our investigation of "mind" in chapter one, we see here again the biblical principle that the direction of our self-consciousness within communal relationships are either directed toward the Creator's intent for us or toward our more animal ("fleshly" and instinctual) orientation. Some developmental psychologists object to such spiritual aspects of moral agency and insist that it is only "nature plus nurture" that determine our concepts of self.

The Christian psychologist Paul Vitz has been writing about the shortfalls of such thinking since the 1970s and in a more recent article explains that these kinds of reductionist ideas ignore the inevitability of the movement to transcendence that is greater than any local or cultural contexts. He writes, "As human beings grow and change and become interpersonally and intellectually more mature, they recognize a process and a trajectory of transcendence in their own life. That is, they come to understand that they have over time transcended—moved beyond and above—their previous self-understanding."[39]

But someone may ask, what about modern neuroscience? What if our experiences are a function of our highly developed brains that have emerged across the millennia to do amazing cognitive feats of perception? It is to that matter that we will now turn.

---

[39] Vitz and Felch, 127.

Chapter 3

THINKING AND THE BRAIN

"WELL, WHAT DO YOU THINK?"

The two friends were just walking away from a session with an enthusiastic preacher who had been encouraging everyone present, "All you need to do is keep up this brain habit for six weeks, and you will be different!"

"I'm not sure," was the reply. "Like, it seems to make sense because the brain is a muscle and training muscles is good."

"Sure," said the friend. "But why are you unsure?" He was genuinely interested.

"Well, I haven't made up my mind yet," he muttered.

"Do you realize you just said you haven't 'made up my mind,' and we have just spent the last hour listening to how to train our brains?" The two stopped and stared at each other.

The second friend started walking again, slowly, and shook his head. "Now I really am confused."

It was a quiet trip home!

IS THE BRAIN ENOUGH?

Another dynamic that has an impact on how we think about thinking is our current use of brain research. Sometimes, it is intended; sometimes, it is implied; and at other times, it is almost accidental. But there can seem to be a suggestion that when we examine the brain, we are seeing the only aspect of our humanity that is involved in thinking.

For example, is our capacity for self-consciousness the result of our highly evolved brains that emerged over time? Similarly, can we explain the ability to know that we know because of the complexity of our neurological processes alone? We will review these questions through two lenses. The first is by considering what some neuroscientists have written. Second, these reflections will take us to facing some philosophical considerations. And we will meet some philosophers who take us again to the concept of embodied souls.

WHAT DOES MODERN BRAIN RESEARCH SUGGEST?

In 1981, D. Gareth Jones brought together some classical and contemporary (for his time) ideas about the brain. His book, *Our Fragile Brains: A Christian Perspective on Brain Research*, reviewed areas that are commonly discussed in such reflections, which included the physical matter that is the brain and its attendant functions. Jones unpacked the mental processes in which we engage that are dependent on the brain, such as language consciousness, behavior, interaction with our environment, and our capacity for the transcendent.[40]

In his last chapter, Jones wrote about the issues which we have been considering—what it means for a Christian in thinking about thinking when we ask ourselves, "What is the role of the brain?" Central to understanding the role of the brain in thinking is what Jones described as "the mind-body problem," which he explained as, "the way we think about states of consciousness on one hand and the states of behavior on the other."[41] In other words, do our actions start in our brains, our self-conscious thinking, or a bit of both? And if it is not all in the brain, then what do we call this other part?

Classically, this often brings the concept of the soul into consideration. Reflecting on the soul as part of our thinking can then lead to debates about whether we are two substances or one. The former is called dualism—and there are different kinds of dualism that have been described—and the latter is called monism—and similarly, there are different kinds of monism that have been described. As Jones summarized, "The problem, at heart, is how to hold together the obvious characteristics of people and their external behavior, and the not-so-obvious characteristics such as their internal mental states."[42] The terms he introduced included the dynamics between the material and immaterial, mind and brain, and between body and soul.

---

40 David Gareth Jones, *Our Fragile Brains: A Christian Perspective on Brain Research* (Westmont: Inter-Varsity Press, 1981).
41 Ibid, 249.
42 Ibid.

Of course, this was not new, even in the 1980s! We could go back to Greek philosophers to engage with some of the earliest records of such reflections. We have already used ancient literature to gain an insight into critical aspects of personhood as it relates to thinking. We saw that in terms of function, the Bible presents our thinking and our mind as having a spiritual direction—either toward the worship of God and loving others or not. Such an orientation (of the heart, as Jesus and the prophets highlighted) has clear implications for the apostle Paul when he explained that in order to reflect deeply on how to live, we must respond to God's mercy.

Biblically, how we live is to be a response to Who God is. For us as Christians, this is the deep heart work that the Bible invites, where "heart" can be thought of as the sum total of who we are before God, which is why Jesus noted that it is what comes out of the heart that demonstrates who we are, not what goes into the stomach (Matt. 15:16-18).

But what Jones was working to summarize some forty years ago is whether this heart work is driven by our brains and whether scientific neurology can demonstrate it. The short answer to both questions is no.

Sir John Eccles, whose earlier work Jones critiqued, won the Nobel Prize for his study of nerve transmission and is one of the neurobiologists who has, for decades, been explaining why the answer to our questions about the brain is no. In the 1987 work, *Mind and Brain: The Many Faceted Problems*, Eccles wrote, "In a sense, mind moves matter in the brain just as an organism moves its component organs and cells."[43]

But Eccles, in exploring the unknowns of the mind-brain interface, also made this observation as a closing comment: "Man has lost his way ideologically in this age . . . I think that science has gone too far in breaking down man's belief in his spiritual greatness . . . the intellectual leaders are too arrogant in their self-sufficiency . . . I come to the belief that we are creatures with some supernatural meaning that is as yet ill defined."[44]

Has this critique been sustained or rebutted in the field of neuroscience in more recent times? That is what we will now examine.

NEUROSCIENCE AND THINKING

The debate above concerning whether humans are only made up of physical matter is not new and has been debated strongly of late by those who believe that brain research has disproved any need for soulness, or the reality of spirituality in our thinking, to explain what our thinking is about. The New Atheists are such a group (e.g., Richard Dawkins, Christopher Hitchens). Prior to them, Stephen Hawkins also worked to find a way of explaining the start of the universe—and thus, the essence of life, including human thinking—that purely relied on the laws of physics.

The Christian psychologist Mark Cosgrove reviewed recent developments in brain research. He gives a generous description of

---

[43] John Eccles, *Mind and Brain: The Many-Faceted Problems* (Icus Books, 1983), 296.
[44] Ibid, 336-37.

what we have learned about the brain but found significant limitations of physicalist assumptions when one reflected on what the human mind can do in contrast to how the brain functions. He notes that:

> The mind is related to but not merely brain areas that are knit together into complex networks ... Personhood is not just about the connections electrically and chemically between multiple brains ... But persons are the message of our active neural and chemical highways, a message we think and feel in our existence every day. The message is our very complicated selves ... We are persons and part of an immaterial reality. This is my guiding, top-down view point.[45]

Similarly to what we have seen already in the previous chapter, Cosgrove argues that we lose a realistic understanding of our mental processes if we do not pay enough attention to consciousness and self-consciousness. He agrees with Thomas Nagel that consciousness is the hard problem that will simply not go away, even with the latest neuroscientific brain-mapping discoveries. Cosgrove ends with a request for researchers to take "a more serious look at human consciousness and self-consciousness."[46]

The Oxford brain scientist, Sharon Dirckx, has reflected this commitment to both the neuroscience and the reality of the unseen aspects of human life. Her 2019 book summarized her research into brain functioning and the nature of human thinking.

---

[45] Mark Cosgrove, *The Brain, the Mind, and the Person Within: The Enduring Mystery of the Soul* (Grand Rapids: Kregel Academic, 2018).
[46] Ibid, 169.

THINKING AND THE BRAIN 51

She noted that when the Bible uses the word *psyche* in explaining that our essence can include the biological she also explained that *psyche* "also goes beyond it."[47] Her research with brains provided a basis to clarify what this looks like. Dirckx outlined how with fMRI scans, we can watch brain activity; but we are not watching someone's actual thoughts. The difference between first and third-person experiences explains the difference: "The scientific method offers third-person observations, whereas conscious experience is encountered in the first-person."[48]

An example from everyday life can help describe this difference. Imagine that a young boy is reported to a senior teacher for throwing a stick out the window of a bus. The senior teacher interviews the student and decides to place him on an in-school detention. The student is also given twenty-four hours to tell his parents before the school contacts them. When the student arrives home, he claims to his mother that he was "only trying to do the right thing and get rid of the stick out of the bus." The mother then promptly sits down and writes a letter of complaint to the senior teacher, outlining that she believed the school had overreacted with the detention.

How are these different opinions being formed? They are both based on external behavior (throwing the stick out the window) and internal report ("I was just trying to help"). In this instance, how was the discrepancy resolved? The starting point was that the adults compared notes about both behavior and their respective

---

47 Sharon Dirckx, *Am I Just My Brain?* (Epsom: The Good Book Company, 2019).
48 Ibid, 45.

discussions. In this case, the mother apologized because even though her son had pleaded innocent internal conscious intentions, he forgot to mention that before throwing the stick out of the window, he had been using it to lift the skirts of girls on the bus.

Such daily experiences—having privileged internal consciousness about our thinking and resulting actions—is why Dirckx went on to highlight that it is the brain that is often responding to the mind. This is consistent with Lennox's explanation of the primacy of spirit over the physical in our universe, and therefore in our natures, because we (humans) are made in the image of God. But Dirckx followed these insights back to biblical principles in a very important area when considering our thinking—the choices that we make.

We, as humans, have agency, which is the freedom to decide what to do with our physical predispositions and capacities coupled with our social contexts (past and present). The very young student in the story above was initially determined to plead his innocence. This was childish moral agency at work. But does such ability exist for its own sake? Dirckx points us back to biblical principles and concluded, "[Christian] philosophers . . . argue that authentic religious experiences more generally are evidence *for* God . . . What's the point of consciousness? *So that we can know God.*"[49] Dirckx thus moved from explaining why our minds are more than our brains to considering *why* we might have this transcendent function in our capacities.

---

49 Ibid, 124.

"Can we [validly] think and speak about God?" Alvin Plantinga commences his book about knowledge and Christian belief.[50] Reflecting on such personal experiences that most of us have, Rod Dreher quoted Solzhenitsyn in his introduction to Trueman's book about how many currently think about themselves and God: "Because men have forgotten God, they have also forgotten man; that's why all this has happened."[51] The events about which Solzhenitsyn was referring were the inhumanities that he had seen and experienced during a totalitarian regime.

WILL COMPUTERS EXPAND OUR BRAINS AND MINDS?

In a related context, exploring whether we can improve our minds with artificial intelligence is an attempted application that is derived from believing that our brains constitute the full nature and experience of our minds. In his book, *2084: Artificial Intelligence and the Future of Humanity*, John Lennox made a gentle nod in response to such a claim undertaken in Orwell's classic apocalyptic novel *1984*. Lennox explored the nature of artificial intelligence (AI) and the claims enthusiasts of AI make about the future. Lennox unpacked his critique by describing biblical teaching about what it means to be human and notes that "matter is not primary but derivative. Spirit is primary.

---

50 Alvin Plantinga, *Knowledge and Christian Belief* (Grand Rapids: W.B. Eerdmans, 2015).
51 Carl Trueman, *The Rise and Triumph of the Modern Self: Cultural Amnesia, Expressive Individualism, and the Road to Sexual Revolution* (Wheaton: Crossway Books, 2020).

Matter does not generate spirit. It is God, who is Spirit, who generates matter."[52]

That is one reason why Lennox explains the impossibility of AI recreating our humanness. "It is an entirely different thing to try to recreate what it feels like to be human [in contrast to mimicking human actions and reactions]. Consciousness bars the way."[53] He also notes that the pursuit for the perfect human through integrated AI is not only impossible but too late. Jesus Christ has already come as the one and only perfect human being. It is why Lennox describes AI attempts at enhancing humans with "technological upgrades" as futile: "The transhumanist *Homo Deus* project could be seen as a parody of this Christian teaching."[54]

SOURCES OF RESPONSIVENESS

Dirckx explained that it was the brain that was often very "responsive to the mind."[55] This is contrary to some narratives that can be heard today. But this is also consistent with the philosophical explanation given by Swinburne, who was introduced earlier. In describing the mind of persons, Swinburne also notes the "privileged" access to first-person thinking that each human has. According to Swinburne, these events are purely mental; and they incorporate what we call beliefs, intentions,

---

52 Lennox, ibid.
53 Ibid, 125.
54 Ibid, 169.
55 Dirckx, 49.

desires, and thoughts (amongst other things). Swinburne outlines his thesis this way:

> Not merely do brain events often cause mental events, but mental events (and in particular intentions) often cause brain events, and therefore bodily movements. Many neuroscientists have interpreted the results of recent neuroscientific experiments as showing that our intentions do not cause brain events. I argue that these results do not show that, and that no experimental results of any kind could possibly show that.[56]

Similarly to the authors already cited, Swinburne follows this line of thinking about thoughts by exploring implications for the uniqueness of our personal agency and responsibility. He notes that because such thoughts are only accessible to the thinker, we (as humans) can never fully predict the moral decisions of another, "Humans (as pure mental substances) cause brain events that cause bodily movements which they intend to cause, and that when they make difficult moral decisions, we will never have enough evidence to predict in advance what they will decide."[57]

NON-REDUCTIVE PHYSICALISTS AND HOLISTIC DUALISTS

Is it time to accept that there are physical and non-physical aspects of reality, or are there still doubts from those who cannot accept the "primacy of spirit" as outlined by Lennox above?

---

56 Swinburne, 2.
57 Ibid, 201.

The question can be put with reference to the cosmos and with reference to persons and their thinking.

Let us review some of the continuing different viewpoints. A non-reductive physicalist can be described as one who believes neither in the soul as a distinct substance or aspect of human existence, but neither do they believe in the reduction of persons to brain states. An example of this would be Brown and Strawn. They note, though, that "the intent of this book is not to present a convincing argument in favour of monism-physicalism, although we present a glimpse," and they hope and "pray we will both get it right as embodied Christian persons." However, they do propose that "due to the incredible complexities of bodies, new properties emerge in human and animal life that transcend, but do not eliminate the rules operating on atoms, molecules and basic biology."[58]

Similarly, Van Inwagen states, "I believe that human persons are material objects (living human organisms), and that they have no part or aspect that is in any way immaterial." However, he makes the following statement after clarifying that he is not a global materialist: "I believe that God exists and God is neither material nor abstract (and no doubt angels, in which I also believe, are concrete things that are not material).[59]

---

58 Warren S. Brown and Brad D. Strawn, *The Physical Nature of the Christian Life: Neuroscience, Psychology, and the Church* (Cambridge: Cambridge University Press, 2012), xii, 6.
59 Peter van Inwagen and Dean Zimmerman, eds. *Persons: Human and Divine* (Oxford: Clarendon Press, 2007), 206.

Thus, Van Inwagen constructed a reality where there is material and non-material realities, but he does not extend his global understanding of reality to the form of persons. He also notes that there are confusions among the dualists but that these do not "infect their central positions." Of the materialists, he notes, "But logical and metaphysical confusion among the materialists amounts to a pandemic."[60]

Similar honesty is noted from another author who is a global materialist—Thomas Nagel, the atheist philosopher previously mentioned. Nagel's focus is the cosmos, but he moves from reviewing the inherent coherency of the explanations of our reality writ large to what that looks like with reference to how people think. He notes that "everyone in our secular culture has been browbeaten into regarding the reductive research program as sacrosanct, on the ground that anything else would not be science.[61]

This does not mean that he wants to admit any form of spiritual being (as does Van Inwagen), even though he did agree that philosophers like Alvin Plantinga have a completely coherent and intelligible philosophy of the cosmos and how people operate within it. Nagel's objections come down to the starting point that he wants to have as a philosopher: ""I confess to an ungrounded assumption of my own, in not finding it possible to regard the design alternative as a real option. I lack the *sensus divnitatis* that enables—indeed compels—so many people to see in the world the

---

60 Ibid.
61 Nagel, 7.

expression of divine purpose as naturally as they see in a smiling face the expression of human feeling."[62]

His quest, when it comes to considerations of the mind, is to find a philosophical middle ground between atheism and the incoherence of neo-Darwinian explanations. "My interest is the territory between them... would an alternative secular conception be possible that acknowledged mind and all that it implies, not as the expression of divine intention but as a fundamental principle of nature along with physical law?"[63]

His initial proposed solution is to start by describing what he calls the "mental nature of the universe," about which he concludes:

> The teleological hypothesis is that these things may be determined ... by a cosmic predisposition to the formation of life, consciousness, and the value that is inseparable from them ... In the present intellectual climate such a possibility is unlikely to be taken seriously, but **I would repeat my earlier observation that no viable account, even a purely speculative one, seems to be available of how a system as staggeringly functionally complex and information rich as a self-reproducing cell, controlled by DNA, RAN or some predecessor, could have arisen by chemical evolution alone from a dead environment**. Recognition of the problem is not limited to the defenders of intelligent design" (emphasis mine).[64]

---

62 Nagel, 12.
63 Ibid, 22.
64 Ibid, 123.

In this, Nagel develops a language that re-defines what physicalism is—that is, his physicalism now includes mentality. A similar trend can be noted from Brown and Strawn when they used the phrase "human and animal life that transcend, but do not eliminate the rules operating on atoms"—that is, while claiming a different understanding of the brain (mind) based on neuropsychological developments, they use a word ("transcend") that inheres a new aspect of the meaning of the word.[65]

Plantinga outlined these issues with reference to the coherence of Christian belief as related to this topic. His project was to explain why materialism is contrary to Christian tradition, and that "even worse (so I'll argue), it is false." His subsequent description is like Swinburne's: "the argument I'll now propose is for the conclusion that no material objects can think—that is, reason and believe, entertain propositions, draw inferences, and the like. But of course I can think; therefore I am not a material object."[66]

Plantinga then focuses on the process of thinking and how this might or might not happen in terms of the brain. Plantinga explains why being a dualist is not a reason to not be "wholly enthusiastic about brain science. The whole issue is nothing but a red herring."[67] It is therefore not surprising that Plantinga said of Cooper's work, "*Body, Soul and Life Everlasting* is careful, thoughtful, and thorough; it provides a much-needed antidote to the facile endorsements of

---

65 Brown and Strawn, ibid.
66 Van Inwagen, 99, 106.
67 Ibid, 123.

mind-body monism so characteristic of contemporary theology and philosophy."[68]

We have noted already John Lennox's explanation that spirit is primary. Or as he explained, "Matter does not generate spirit. It is God, who is Spirit, who generates matter."[69] Lennox came to this clarification after considering our soulness, and possible materialistic worldviews, which he summarised as follows:

> Distinguished Christian philosophers Alvin Plantinga, Richard Swinburne, and J.P. Moreland argue that we shall make no real progress in understanding until we are prepared to revive an ongoing thoroughgoing substance dualism—that is, to recognize that there is a non-physical aspect to human beings. Even philosopher David Chalmers, who specializes in this area, though he is strongly inclined to materialism, argues, "Reductive explanation of consciousness is impossible and I even argue for a kind of dualism."[70]

So, given what we have reviewed so far from the Bible, philosophers, and neuroscientists about our thinking minds, what might be some implications for how we can live?

---

68 Ibid.
69 Lennox, 125.
70 Ibid, 125.

Chapter 4
THINKING AND CHARACTER

AMY WAS CLEARLY DISTRESSED AS she and her good friend walked along together. Summer was not sure how to support her.

"It was just so unfair!" Amy declared. "He should never have asked that question . . ."

Summer was not sure if Amy was going to explode with anger or simply cry.

"What would you have preferred?" asked Summer, being a person who liked to move forward at moments like these.

"Well, he should have said nothing about it—his identity markers don't give him the right." Amy was now calmer and working to be thoughtful.

"What do you mean by 'identity markers'?" Summer had an idea of what her friend meant but wanted to double check.

"For a start, he's a man, and white, and probably married to a woman," was the reply.

"And remind me—why does that mean he can't ask a question about being trans?" Again, Summer had her suspicions but thought it wise to hear her friend speak out her ideas.

"Because his class of people have had it all their own way and do not have the right to speak of things outside their experience, that's why." Amy expressed all this with reasserted confidence.

"Hmm," mused Summer. "So does that mean we should not speak about men's issues because we are women—perhaps only when it affects us?"

"Maybe," was the short reply.

"Does that include that messy one at college at the moment— you know, about transwomen who have biological male advantage competing in our swimming competitions next week, where they will win and we will lose?" Summer just realized this theoretical discussion was becoming real for her and her swimming buddy.

"But they are women, not men," Amy replied, seeing a way through.

"Then why did we both agree it was unfair for them to compete against us just yesterday, claiming they were 'not woman enough'?" Summer was now working hard to make sense of it all.

Amy stopped walking and stood still to think. "You know, I don't know. It all seems too hard."

"And on that we can agree," said Summer.

And they walked again, arm in arm, seeking reassurance about what was real for them in their lives.

HOW CAN WE THINK ABOUT CHARACTER?

Earlier on in this little book, we noted that a good theory or idea helps us explain reality better. That led us to reflecting on the nature of reality and the biblical claim that there are seen and unseen aspects of human life and that the latter (spirit) has primacy over the former (matter). How might that help when facing the kinds of dilemmas that Amy and Summer were confronting?

Two authors wrote an interesting book called *The Coddling of the American Mind* about patterns of thinking that can confuse us when wrestling with such issues. They describe what they believe are three aspects of reality being taught to our young people and label these patterns of thinking "The Three Great Untruths." They describe these three relational difficulties as:

- The Untruth of Fragility: *what doesn't kill you makes you weaker.*
- The Untruth of Emotional Reasoning: *always trust your feelings.*
- The Untruth of Us Versus Them: *life is a battle between good people and evil people.*[71]

In response to each of these "untruths," they propose alternatives which can be summarized as:

- It is good to struggle, in order to develop as a person (within some limits of course).
- While emotions or affections are important in understanding ourselves and others, we also need to be able to reason when considering difficult issues.

---

71 Lukianoff, 4.

- Quoting Alexandr Solzhenitsyn, they suggested that good and evil runs through the hearts of all of us, which means that if someone disagrees with us, that does not automatically mean that they are evil.[72]

But here is a further interesting question—what were the criteria these authors used to decide what is a great untruth? Lukianoff and Haidt were refreshingly transparent about their choices. They said:

> While many propositions are untrue, in order to be classified as a Great Untruth, an idea must meet three criteria:
>
> - It contradicts ancient wisdom (ideas found widely in the wisdom literature of many cultures).
> - It contradicts modern psychological research on well-being.
> - It harms the individuals and communities who embrace it"[73]

In using such criteria, Lukianoff and Haidt demonstrate the belief that we human beings have the capacity to make choices in our minds. As they describe it:

---

72 Ibid.
73 Ibid, 4.

> We are saying that what people choose to *do* in their heads will determine how those real problems affect them . . . [To avoid the Great Untruths] means *seeking out challenges* (rather than eliminating or avoiding everything that "feels unsafe"), *freeing yourself from cognitive distortions* (rather than always trusting your initial feelings), and *taking a generous view of other people, and looking for nuance* (rather than assuming the worst about people within a simplistic us-versus-them morality).[74]

Is this kind of advice enough on which to build our ideas of good or bad in terms of patterns for our thinking and subsequent behavior? How we answer this question is important because this kind of decision-making—and what we subsequently put into action because of what we do in our heads—is the basis of our character. We can further ask about the implications of using these kinds of criteria given what we have seen from the biblical concerns about thinking. For example, does it lead us to love God and others more? Lukianoff and Haidt's work looks to have some practical wisdom to it (we *can* ask ourselves whether we can see these patterns of untruth in our world, and we may conclude yes or no). And even though they do look back to "ancient wisdom" (which can be rare for current-day social scientists), they appear to come short of a satisfactory metaphysic. That is, there is no certainty for testing whether thinking is good, poor, or evil.

---

74 Ibid, 14.

WHO SAYS WHAT GOOD CHARACTER IS?

Why does our thinking need some certainty for our character to be good? Our exploration in chapter one clearly identified that intentional thinking reflects the state of our hearts, and it indicates whether our desire is to know God more or not. As the apostle John outlined in his first epistle, this also reflects whether our desire is to love others more or not (1 John 2:9-11).

What, then, does the Bible say is the way to grow more mature in our thinking, which in turn will be reflected in displaying a more mature character? Interestingly, if you try to find the word "character" in the older translations of the Bible, you will not find it.[75] However, you will find the word with reference to who we are as people in newer translations in a couple of instances. Does this difference mean that there has been a general shift in how we think about character, or might it be that using this language reflects that we now know more about personhood?

In chapter one, we noted a couple of instances where biblical translation can shift because contemporary ideas about who we are do not easily accept the unseen reality of spirituality with reference to our thinking—and thus "attitude" was used in translations instead of "spirit" or even "mind." The use of such personality language can represent a reorientation of our thinking. Where once we might explore right and wrong questions before God (in fellowship with others), we can now

---

[75] The exception is for when it is used not in terms of who we are as a person but for the kind of lettering of a document, as in Isaiah 8:1.

see (in the media and our educational institutions) a strong push toward self-orientation: self-help, self-esteem, self-fulfilment, self-potential—noting that such language has increased dramatically since the 1960s.

A Christian psychologist (briefly mentioned earlier) who has critiqued this pressure within psychology for decades is Professor Emeritus Paul C. Vitz. The title of his earliest book in the area gives a hint about the problem he saw arising back in the 1970s: *Psychology as Religion: The Cult of Self-worship.* Vitz basically notes that there had been a shift in the study of people that moved more strongly toward a focus on the study of self as the basis for considering what was good or not for personhood.[76]

In a much later publication, Vitz further explains how even though the presuppositions of secular psychology remain unstated, they have had a continuing dramatic impact on how they conceptualize what it means to be a person. In abandoning the starting premise that "God exists, and that He is a person with whom one is in relationship,"[77] much of contemporary psychology has become deterministic, morally relativistic, and subjective.

Each of these three terms reflects the absence of God in our thinking (as the apostle Paul pointed out in Romans 1). Determinism is the belief that life is prescribed by our inherited genetic capacity

---

76 Paul C. Vitz, *Psychology as Religion: The Cult of Self-worship* (Grand Rapids: Eerdmans Publishing, 1977).
77 Vitz, "Chapter 4: Modern Personality Theories: A Critical Understanding of Personality from a Catholic Christian Perspective," in *A Catholic Christian Met-Model of the Person: Integration with Psychology and Mental Health Practice* (Sterling: Divine Mercy University Press, 2020), 63.

and predispositions, plus our social contexts past and present. In chapter one, we noted that this is in contrast to the emphasis that the Bible places on our hearts, which, as Jesus taught, is the seat of who we are before God and thus our character.[78]

Moral relativism is what Lukianoff and Haidt describe in their second great untruth. Basically, it is when we decide what is right and wrong without reference to our Creator God's will for us (Gen. 3:1-7). The current manifestation of this dynamic, if Lukianoff and Haidt (and others) are right, is that we are encouraged to always place priority on trusting our feelings (emotions).

Subjectivism is the extension of moral relativism. It is the "expressionism" of which MacIntyre warned (see later in this chapter). In this mode of thinking, we not only make decisions primarily on our feelings, but we also deny that there are any other criteria that can be applied to us.

This kind of social agreement about how to think about right and wrong, or character, demonstrates that psychology's explorations generally are no longer responsive to what C. S. Lewis described as *Tao*,[79] or as "natural law," based on the common grace theology of Romans 1, Psalm 19, and Psalm 24. These passages explain that the presence of our Creator God can be seen by any honest observer of the nature of our world. The extension of belief in a Creator is that we are made to live in a certain way (sometimes

---

[78] For example, Matthew 12:34 and Matthew 15:11.
[79] C. S. Lewis, *The Abolition of Man* (Glasgow: Collins Fount Paperbacks, 1982 edition).

called "natural theology"). This way of life, which can also be called the "virtuous life," is directed, according to Scripture, toward love of God and of others.

SHIFTING TO THE THERAPEUTIC

Some have labeled this shift as a move toward a "therapeutic" mindset, rather than a God-oriented mindset. Philip Rieff used this term in 1966 and describes, similarly to Lewis, the loss of reference to God when considering how to live as a human being. However, he also describes the nature of the replacement idea—that the center of personhood was now not only the self but also a form of the self that was committed to having "nothing at stake beyond a manipulative sense of well-being. This is the unreligion of the age, and its master [is] science."[80]

The use of the term "unreligion" became a theme of Rieff's book, as he continued to compare and contrast what was the more established tradition of accepting biblical principles of self to the movement to the new industry of self-fulfilment. In the more traditional mode of thought, acceptance of needing saving meant that one could experience forgiveness and grace, which could lead to loving others more fully (in view of God's mercy, as the apostle Paul reminds us in Romans 12:1). In the therapeutic mindset, "our culture has shifted toward a predicate of impulse release, projecting

---

[80] Philip Rieff, *The Triumph of the Therapeutic: Uses of Faith After Freud 40th Anniversary Edition* (Wilmington: ISI Books, 2007), 10.

controls unsteadily based upon an infinite variety of wants raised to the status of need."[81]

Lewis calls this shift the "abolition of man [mankind]." Rieff labels it the beginning of "anti-culture." His reasoning is that before the current era in Western culture, it was assumed that human beings—slowly and sometimes stubbornly—were becoming more tolerant personally and socially because they had an eye on their own possibilities (being made in the image of God and each worthy of respect) and also because they had an eye on their brokenness (being sinners in need of help to control their baser desires). Rieff described that to ignore the former increased the risk of undoing aspects of culture that enabled growing mutual commitments.

Another voice that highlighted this dilemma was Alasdair MacIntyre.[82] Similarly to Rieff and others, he noted that shifts away from God and community often result in the rise of individualism. That is, MacIntyre, like others before him, notes that without a center bigger and stronger than individuals who are looking out for themselves, the tendency is for a weakening of relationships at the interpersonal and social levels. The corollary to this shift is that it also opens up the way for new social structures, wherein the "locus of expertise" also shifts away from the religious teachers and leaders. Rieff notes, like Chesterton in the 1920s, that the replacements for God-focused teachers have been the "people

---

81 Ibid, p.13.
82 MacIntyre, ibid.

of science of the self." MacIntyre describes this dynamic as a movement to a culture of emotivism. He summarizes his thesis as, "I am not merely contending that morality is not what it once was, but also and more importantly that what once was morality has to some large degree disappeared—and that this marks a degeneration, a grave cultural loss."[83]

The reasons that this shift creates a "degeneration" are that there are no longer any "ultimate criteria" on which people can agree about right and wrong and that relationships in themselves, therefore, tend to be pragmatic, rather than what some theologians would call "covenantal." In covenantal relationships, we are called to commit to others in order to do good to and with them before God. In pragmatic relationships, "each person treats the other primarily as a means to his or her ends."[84]

WHY WE NEED A GOOD METAPHYSIC

In the third edition of his work, MacIntyre describes, with refreshing transparency, what he believes is missing from his initial analysis, which was a metaphysic. Metaphysics helps us talk about the very basics of what is real, what is there, and what it is like. When I wrote in the first chapter that a starting point for thinking about thinking is that "God is there," that is a metaphysical statement. It becomes a starting point which cannot be proved by scientific method. It is a statement of trust that helps

---

83 Ibid, 22.
84 Ibid, 23.

us understand reality better. That starting point creates a certain basis for the rest of our thinking, if we accept it. It is why the Bible makes statements such as, "The fear of the Lord is the beginning of wisdom" (Prov. 9:10) and that our thinking can be futile or wise depending on whether we accept and act on God's revealed Word (Rom. 1:21; Psalm 14:1).

MacIntyre realized that without such an anchor for deciding what is good in society, morality (and thus character) can become reduced to whatever the "crowd" decided. He expresses it this way:

> But I had now learned from Aquinas that my attempt to provide an account of the human good purely in social terms, in terms of practices, traditions, and the narrative unity of human lives, was bound to be inadequate until I had provided it with a metaphysical grounding. It is only because human beings have an end toward which they are directed by reason of their specific nature, that practices, tradition and the like are able to function as they do.[85]

Christians believe we are oriented toward self-consciousness and transcendent thinking that enables us to know God and worship Him and to love others. As MacIntyre and others have described it, the movement away from that foundational belief results in other ends vying for our attention and commitments. And the mode of this competition for our attention is feeling-focused—what Lukianoff and Haidt call "the untruth of emotional

---

85   Ibid, xi.

reasoning," what Vitz calls "worship of self," and what MacIntyre calls "emotivism." "Whatever criteria or principles or evaluative allegiances the emotivist self may profess, they are to be construed as expressions of attitudes, preferences and choices which are themselves not governed by criterion, principle of value, since they underlie and are prior to all allegiance to criterion, principle or value."[86]

When these patterns of thought occur in a society, it means that we have trouble agreeing with what is good character and what is not. Loss of agreement on what is good also means that we have more difficulty understanding each other and, sometimes, more difficulty in disagreeing with each other respectfully. It is our senses (feelings and sensual emotions) that drive us and not a desire to live as we were made to live.

WHITHER CHARACTER?

Such emotivist thinking and resultant action could be used as a contemporary example of the dynamics behind the secularization (or denial of God) that the apostle Paul outlined in Romans 1. Before that, let us look at another description of the loss of capacity to understand the basis of good character, given to us by the sociologist James Davison Hunter.[87] Hunter undertook a historical overview of the conceptualizing of character from

---

86 Ibid, 33.
87 Stephen J. Fyson, "Character, Oh! Character, Where Art Thou?," *Teach* 10, no. 2 (November 2016): 29-34. https://research.avondale.edu.au/cgi/viewcontent.cgi?article=1324&context=teach.

a sociological perspective and attempted to summarize how different approaches to teaching character have had different impacts on young people. He noted that in the 1800s and earlier 1900s in America and much of the West, "character was always related to an explicitly moral standard of conduct. While the word 'character' did not disappear, an alternative vision of the self-emerged. This vision was captured by the word 'personality' . . . The concept of personality reflected a self no longer defined by austerity but by emancipation for the purposes of expression, fulfilment, and gratification."[88]

Hunter notes the introduction of a focus on personality, as previously described by Vitz. What aspects of our thinking about character may be affected by this shift toward the concept of personality? As we have already seen, there are important changes that occur in how we decide in our thinking about what is right and wrong if we move from understanding our Creator's thoughts (by knowing Him) to determining our own character criteria through relativistic social interactions. To unpack this dynamic further, Hunter also traces what happened to how young people were taught about virtue and vices in the invitation to grow in their character.

The following table is how I summarized Hunter's historical overview:[89]

---

[88] James Davison Hunter, *The Death of Character: Moral Education in an Age Without Good or Evil* (New York City: Basic Books, 2000), 7.
[89] Fyson, ibid.

Aspect of Character Development	From	To
Content of Moral Instruction	The "objective" moral truths of Divine Scriptures and the laws of nature	The conventions of a democratic society, to the subjective values of the individual person
Sources of Moral Authority	From a transcendent God	To the institutions of the natural order and the scientific paradigms that sustain them, to the choices of subjects
Sanctions	From the institutions and codes of the community	To the sovereign choices of the autonomous individual
Primary Institutional Location	The family and local religious congregation and the youth organizations	The public school and popular culture
Arbiters of Moral Judgement	The clergyman	The psychologist and counselor

Character of Moral Pedagogy	The cultivation of a sense of good and evil through memorization of sacred texts	To a largely emotive deliberation over competing values
Premise of Moral Education	The sense that people are, for all their other endearments, sinful and rebellious	To a sense that they are good by nature and only need encouragement
Purpose of Moral Education	Mastery over the soul in service of God and neighbor	The training of character to serve the needs of civic life, to the cultivation of personality toward the end of well-being

Hunter's conclusion about our current situation in terms of how we think and teach about character is that all the major paradigms now are "at root, self-referencing and oriented toward the end of personal well-being."[90] One area of life where this is clearly seen is in how we think about relationships, generally, and intimacy, particularly.

---

90 Ibid, 147.

This is not the place to describe the many faceted aspects of this foundational shift in our thinking, and other people have already done that well. One such author is Carl Trueman, and we will turn to him to help summarize how the movement away from biblical understandings of thinking have underpinned the acceptance of alternative descriptions of what life should be like.

THINKING ABOUT THE SELF TODAY

Trueman uses the work of Philip Rieff, Charles Taylor, and Alasdair McIntyre to highlight that one of the most significant shifts that has occurred in our current era in the West is a focus on highly individualized sexual identities. It is worth noting that while God reveals to us in the Bible a very particular pattern of relationships, including intimacy between a man and woman, our Western world has shifted to the loss of truth and, thus, character.

Trueman highlights that the basis of the current debates is competing ideas about anthropology—or how we think about the nature of persons. We have seen that the Bible clearly presents our natures as embodied souls made in the image of God but fallen and broken and in need of saving in order to live together as our Creator God intended. As Trueman summarizes, "All human beings are made in the image of God. But in the current climate, this universal dignity has been psychologized, and the granting of dignity has come to be equated with the affirmation of those psychologized identities that enjoy special status in our culture."[91]

---

91 Trueman, 331.

Therefore, in our current era and within the antitheism described by Taylor, the therapeutic style focus on individualized wellbeing outlined by Rieff, and the emotivist basis for moral decision-making presented by McIntyre, we have come to a world where our individual sexual identity is the most sacrosanct aspect of life. "Before Freud, sex was an activity, for procreation or for recreation; after Freud, sex is definitive of who we are, as individuals, as societies, and as a species."[92]

Such a way of thinking about our character, in terms of who we are in relationship with others, has enormous consequences for education. "Where a sense of psychological well-being is the purpose of life, therapy supplants morality—or, perhaps better, therapy is morality—and anything that achieves that sense of well-being is good."[93]

And it is to these applied issues we will turn in the next chapter after briefly reviewing two more Bible passages about how to think about who we are.

A QUICK BIBLICAL REFLECTION

Two other biblical verses reinforce what we have noted so far. When it comes to thinking (in the intentional causation sense described by Swinburne), the Bible is always interested in our direction. Is our thinking drawing us closer to God and others, or not?

---

[92] Ibid, 221.
[93] Ibid, 360.

The same is true in verses where the original language words are translated as "character." These two examples highlight this consistent pattern in meaning—Romans 5:4 and 1 Corinthians 15:33. In the Romans context, the apostle Paul is explaining how Christians have accessed the grace of Christ through faith. But this faith is not static; Christians mature as they walk the path of faith. At times, this requires persevering so that we become stronger (unlike the safetyism that comes from the untruth of the myth of fragility). Paul links suffering, perseverance, character, and hope which does not disappoint because of the work of the Holy Spirit.

This rendering of "character" is not based on personality. What the Bible emphasizes is whether or not one's life is oriented toward God. That is why in passages like this, the point of experiencing suffering is to draw the Christian to the reality of God's hope in Christ through the Holy Spirit. This is very different to the shift described above that leads to increased individualistic emotivism where self-fulfilment is the central focus.

Similarly in 1 Corinthians 15:33, the apostle Paul quotes a Greek poet to encourage those in the Christian church in Corinth to come back to their senses in understanding the centrality of the resurrection of Christ to the Gospel. The New International Version has the phrase as, "Do not be misled: 'Bad company corrupts good character.'" The older King James Version has it as, "Be not deceived: evil communications corrupt good manners." Again, the concept of "character" was not known in the KJV times, and the intent of the passage was to remind Christians about whether the influences around them drew them to God, or not. "Good manners" indicates a public expression of who we are by how we act. The English Standard Version is more direct with this implication: "Do not be deceived: 'Bad company ruins good morals.'"

These passages, when we see them in their fuller original meanings, demonstrate how we have lost so much of what the Bible teaches us about character. We look to feel good all the time—the Bible teaches us to grow in the hard times towards a deeper hope in Christ. We look to make up our own minds about feeling good about ourselves—the Bible teaches us to review our manners and morals in light of what God has revealed to us through His Word and Christ.

WHERE ARE WE UP TO?

In this chapter we have reviewed how our thinking about character has shifted from being accountable and supported in our moral decision-making before God and others to being focused only on self-well-being and flourishing. The trouble with this individualistic emotivism is that it leads to relationships with others that are less human because of fewer reconciled relationships with God. This is an example of what happens when our thinking does not start with God.

The next chapter will give further case studies about how this happens with reference to contemporary education, as based on godless and self-focused relativistic and emotivist (sentimental) psychology. This will be contrasted to what the Bible describes as "renewing our minds" (Rom. 12:2).

Chapter 5

THINKING AND LEARNING

"HEY, DID YOU SEE THIS quote from Richard Dawkins?" asked the young but ultra-keen science student.

"Which one was that?" replied his patient friend, who was more focused on understanding the implicit themes within Shakespeare's *Romeo and Juliet*.

"Well, there is this one about men and women being men and women because of biology—or sex being binary, as he put it. But then he said you have more choice with race." The science student was being cautious in case others were listening and did not understand the context.

"Oh, what did he say?" The Shakespearean student was now interested.

"'Race is very much a spectrum . . . Most African-Americans are mixed race, so there really is a spectrum. Somebody who looks white may even call themselves black, may have a very slight [inheritance]. People who have one great-grandparent who is Native American may call themselves Native American. Sex, on the other hand, is pretty . . . binary. So on the face of it, it would seem easier for someone to identify as whatever race they choose. If you have one black parent and one white parent, you might think you could choose what to identify as.'"[94]

"What? So, is Dawkins saying that it is okay to name any race that might be in your background, but there are limits when it comes to gender identity?" The Shakespearean student was starting to think around plotlines for her next piece of drama writing.

"It appears so." The science student was still ruminating.

"Did it cause him any problems when he said this?" The literature major was testing for other storylines.

"Apparently, he lost his 1996 Humanist of the Year award from the American Humanist Association. So yes, it cost him, and it seems to have disappointed him." This made the science student uneasy about his fellow scientists.

"Hmmm. Do we know how he made sense of all this—a world leading scientist at Oxford being disowned by other scientists?" Reconciliation is often the resolution that writers seek.

"From what I read, it seems that he is looking for more transparency and openness among scientists and maybe even

---

94 Josh Glancy, "How Cancel Culture Clipped Dawkins' Wings," The Weekend Australian Magazine online, November 12, 2021, https://www.theaustralian.com.au/subscribe/news/1/?sourceCode=TAWEB_WRE170_a&dest=https%3A%2F%2Fwww.theaustralian.com.au%2Fweekend-australian-magazine%2Fcancel-culture-clips-richard-dawkins-wings%2Fnews-story%2F665af37f529883923a73134998c27f5c&memtype=anonymous&mode=premium&v21=dynamic-groupb-test-noscore&V21spcbehaviour=append.

humility. He reportedly said, 'It's important to state what we [scientists] don't know . . . We don't know what dark matter is,[sic] we don't know how the universe started and how life started. We don't understand consciousness. We mustn't fall into the trap of being seen as arrogant because we think we know everything. We're working on it.'"[95]

The young scientist stood still and reflected and then suggested, "I don't think I have ever heard one of my science lecturers talk about consciousness. Perhaps I should ask about our capacity for self-consciousness and, from that, what it means to be a person and then, maybe, about the meaning of life . . ."

"Ah, that almost sounded like an invitation to poetry," said his friend with a smile.

"Don't be silly," he said as they sat in the library, pondering.

SOME FURTHER BIBLICAL REFLECTIONS

A repeated theme in this book has stated that for us human beings, thinking is distinctive. The very act of thinking reminds us that there are more than physical aspects of reality. These unseen realities have important implications for what we do with our thinking. Do we, in the apostle Paul's terms, renew our minds in Christ or not? Or in Augustine's terms (quoting Christ), do we seek love of God and others more or not?

---
95   Ibid.

THE MIND OF CHRIST

> *"'For who has understood the mind of the Lord so as to instruct him?' But we have the mind of Christ."*
>
> 1 Corinthians 2:16

If we believe we are not spiritual beings but just physical, then this verse will never make sense. The apostle Paul met Jesus on the road to Damascus, and his life was transformed. As part of that transformation, he understood Who Christ is and then understood that to believe in Him was to see the whole world differently. There was nothing he thought about that would not go through the "renewal process" to avoid "futile thinking" (Eph. 4:17) from a "debased mind" (Rom. 1:28).

Because we are spiritual and Jesus has sent His Holy Spirit to be with those who believe in Him, Paul's claim here is logical—we can have the mind of Christ. Having this mind is not a static process, as the next couple of verses demonstrate.

THINKING IS ABOUT RENEWAL

> *I appeal to you therefore, brothers and sisters, by the mercies of God, to present your bodies as a living sacrifice, holy and acceptable to God, which is your spiritual worship Do not be conformed to this world, but be transformed by the renewal of your mind, that by testing you may discern what is the will of God, what is good and acceptable and perfect.*
>
> Romans 12:1-2

When our thinking starts with God, we respond with awe and thanks for Who He is and what He has done (and is doing); or alternatively, as seen in Romans 1:18-23, we take His good gifts, play with them, and ignore the Giver of those gifts. But when we accept Who God is as the Giver, we respond by wanting to live by using our gifts in helping others (1 Peter 4:10). This is our "logical service" or "reasonable worship."

How do we know what is good for others in response to God? Biblically, we can see that our minds need renewal so that we do not fall into the God-denying patterns of thought that can arise at any time. Such no-God patterns of thinking can dominate within a subject discipline and its connected professions, such as education's use (some would say reliance upon) of psychology.

THE MIND OF CHRIST IS FOR ALL OUR THOUGHTS

"For though we walk in the flesh, we are not waging war according to the flesh. For the weapons of our warfare are not of the flesh but have divine power to destroy strongholds. We destroy arguments and every lofty opinion raised against the knowledge of God, and take every thought captive to obey Christ."

2 Corinthians 10:3-5

Sometimes, we use the phrase that we "wrestle with our thoughts." In this part of Paul's letter, we can see the biblical intent of such a process. Our thinking either thankfully acknowledges all good gifts that always come "from above" (James 1:17), or it is focused on our self-belonging, as Alan Noble described it. Paul's encouragement asks his readers to refocus so that none of their thinking shifts away from God so that they can do the good He has prepared for them to do (Eph. 2:8-10).

THE FOCUS OF MIND-RENEWAL IS LOVE

> *"Now concerning food offered to idols: we know that 'all of us possess knowledge.' This 'knowledge' puffs up, but love builds up."*
>
> 1 Corinthians 8:1

When our knowledge is divorced from the reality of God, we attribute all our giftings and achievements to ourselves. This is what Alan Noble has explained with his term "self-belonging," which means we use our capacities and activities to reinforce that "we are our own." Noble unpacks that when we use our abilities to reinforce that we can successfully take "responsibility for self-belonging," we tire out ourselves or pretend we are successful within it.[96] Such an analysis reflects what Paul says in this verse—we can all have this kind of "knowledge" (to reinforce our self-belonging), but it inflates us. Love of God and others, however, builds up others according to their needs.

That is why thinking that starts with God makes a difference in our relational lives. A clear explanation of Paul's

---

96 Alan Noble, *You Are Not Your Own: Belonging to God in an Inhuman World* (Westmont: InterVarsity Press, 2021).

description of this relationship between our thinking and living (Rom. 1:16-32) is found in Nancey Pearcey's *Finding Truth*. Pearcey encourages us to develop some spiritual self-discipline in our thinking by:

1. Identifying the idol in our thinking when we ignore our Creator God
2. Describing the subsequent reductionism in thinking that occurs when we ignore God
3. Exploring how an idol-based way of thinking contradicts the observable facts that are given to everyone through general revelation
4. Noting how the ideology collapses in on itself because it is reductionist and rejects observable life knowledge
5. Learning to articulate the coherency of biblical truths.[97]

We will use these five principles to test out the dominant paradigm that educational psychology uses to explain teaching and learning—that of personhood being describable and predictable through the dual lens of nature and nurture (building on the earlier comments of Vitz).

---

[97] Nancy Pearcey, *Finding Truth: 5 Principles for Unmasking Atheism, Secularism, and Other God Substitutes* (Colorado Springs: David Cook Books, 2015).

THE PSYCHOLOGY BEHIND CONTEMPORARY EDUCATION

IDENTIFYING THE IDOL IN OUR THINKING WHEN WE IGNORE OUR CREATOR GOD

We often hear the phrase "the research says." And surely we can trust "the research." After all, we have many Christian psychologists who help Christian teachers. Surely, there are kernels of truth in these statements.

However, as St. Augustine noted, any teaching by a Christian that is not focused on the "two loves" will end in ultimate futility (lack of wisdom). Those two loves are simply "love of God and love of others."[98]

Has this been the focus of psychology? We cannot do a full review of the field here, but as noted previously, some authors have worked to summarize what has happened when psychology has ignored God. Another early critique of psychology described its no-God heritage this way:

> In the beginning were Wisdom and Confusion. And they begat Humanism, who lived one thousand years, begetting sons and daughters. Humanism begat Empiricism, who married Evolution, and they begat Old Psychology. Old Psychology lived only thirty years and begat three children: Behaviourism, who married Brain Research, both of whom were very neat and proper; Humanistic Psychology, a kindly

---

98 Augustine, ibid.

child named after its grandfather; and Transpersonal Psychology, who was a very odd child indeed.[99]

Cosgrove went on to explain five inadequacies of psychology, summarizing the difficulties that arise from this history of psychology: "What should be rejected is the view that *all* human problems will be solved by some chemical, behavioural or meditative technique."[100]

That is, one idolatry that is common in Western society is that we can fix any personal problems (relational or learning) with psychology that is based on secular humanism and the scientific method. We need nothing from God, His revelation, or His Son. In this line of thinking, psychology's self-focus has resulted in the idolatry of selfism: we are the center of our worlds; and when in trouble, we can get ourselves out of trouble. It is why Vitz's book that we mentioned earlier was subtitled *The Cult of Self-Worship.*

Other more recent authors have also explained what this looks like. Theodore Dalrymple, in explaining this idolatry, describes that such a stance also has direct consequences for how we practise our morality:

> But the overall effect of psychological thought on human culture and society, I contend, has been overwhelmingly negative because it gives the false impression of greatly increased human self-understanding where it not has been achieved, it

---
99 Mark Cosgrove, *Psychology Gone Awry* (Westmont: InterVarsity Press, 1982), 17.
100 Ibid, 131.

> encourages the evasion of responsibility by turning subjects into objects where it supposedly takes account of or interests itself in subjective experiences, and it makes shallow the human character because it discourages genuine self-examination and self-knowledge. It is ultimately sentimental and promotes the grossest self-pity, for it makes everyone (apart from scapegoats) victims of their own behaviour.[101]

What Dalrymple calls unachieved (or pretend) self-understanding is the subtle but pervasive idolatry that is dominant in the worlds of psychology and education. It is often hidden in the language of self-actualization, or achieving self-potential, or being the "best me" that I can be. Clearly, the Bible verses we have reviewed to date do not support our minds being renewed without God's Holy Spirit. But our world is in many ways convinced otherwise. How can anyone recognize the work of the Holy Spirit when non-physical aspects of reality are being ignored?

Sadly, even Christians working in psychology and education can do so in this "fractured" mindset. That is, they have a Christian view of salvation, Christian spiritual habits, and even some Christian morality. But they do not know how to think as a Christian outside of these spaces.[102] It is why some suggest that we cannot speak into the "big picture" issues of our time as Christians, even while continuing to grieve about what is happening in our

---

[101] Theodore Dalrymple *Admirable Evasions: How Psychology Undermines Morality* (New York: Encounter Books, 2015), 112.

[102] Harry Blamires, *The Christian Mind: How Should a Christian Think?* (London: Regent College Publishing, 2005).

times. As we saw above, Carl Trueman explains this with reference to how we think about ourselves. The opening question of his book summarizes this conundrum well: "The origins of this book lie in my curiosity about how and why a particular statement has come to be regarded as coherent and meaningful: 'I am a woman trapped in a man's body.'"[103]

If we believe we belong to ourselves, we are idolatrous before God. If we believe we can live in a way that ignores God's realities, we are idolatrous before Him. If we believe that any discussion and thinking about God in psychology and education is like putting unnecessary clutter in a sitting room, then we are being idolatrous. It is easy to see this misguided self-sufficiency within psychology and education. That is because of the inherent reductionism that has captured psychology as applied to education in our current era.

DESCRIBING THE SUBSEQUENT REDUCTIONISM IN THINKING THAT OCCURS WHEN WE IGNORE GOD

Psychiatrist Thomas Szasz, warned of this difficulty of confusing what was and what was not an issue of the soul. He was concerned that denial of our soulness would confuse psychiatrists in their work. He recognized that working with people involved understanding physical aspects of reality (the brain) and unseen aspects of reality (the soul). The latter, he posited, is not open to medicine because it is not understandable by the natural scientific method.

---

103 Trueman, 19.

Like Dalrymple decades later, Szasz saw that this shift was away from the religious to the secular humanistic frame of mind and that this had dire consequences for understanding moral conduct. As we have seen from Vitz, Trueman, and Noble, this is because moral conduct focused on the self does not sustain mutual relationships. As with all idolatrous claims that replace the rightful place of the Creator God with some human substitute, there arises an incompleteness because what is under investigation is ultimately reductionist. Szasz uses the language of replacing the constructs of "religious-humanistic" frameworks with "dehumanized pseudo-medical" ones.[104] He called this the "lie" of how we think about the concept of "mental illness":

> The claim that "mental illnesses are diagnosable disorders of the brain" is not based on scientific research; it is a lie, an error, or a naïve revival of the somatic premise of the long-discredited humoral theory of disease... Mental illness is a metaphor. Minds can be "sick" only in the sense that jokes are "sick" or economies are "sick"... Mental illness is not something a person has but is something he does or is.[105]

Notice that Szasz is identifying the reductionistic move to equate "mind" with "brain." We have seen that biblically, the two are distinct but work as a unit, as philosophers like Swinburne have explained. Szasz then goes on to describe how this initial

---
104 Thomas Szasz, *The Myth of Mental Illness: Foundations of a Theory of Personal Conduct* (New York: Harper Perennial, 2010), xiv.
105 Ibid, xii, 267.

reductionism reduces our moral responsibility as humans in social interactions: "There are no more bad people in the world; there are only mentally ill people. The 'insanity defense' annuls misbehavior, the sin of yielding to temptation, and tragedy."[106]

Earlier, we noted that many psychologists use two dynamics of life to research whatever it is they are interested in studying. "Nature" represents our physically inherited predispositions and capacities. For example, I am a short man. Doing well in high jump was never going to be an option for me. Our physical capacities do matter.

"Nurture" summarizes our social contexts, past and present. My father taught me to be a man of my word. My mother encouraged me that it was what was on the inside that counts. Social contexts do matter.

I have argued that a clearer description of our reality is that we are embodied souls. Without this soulness, we miss describing crucial parts of who we are and how we think. Genetics-only determination combined with understanding social-upbringing would make us only animals. I have contended that as embodied souls, we have the capacity to choose what to do with our genetic predispositions and our social starts to life.

For example, Spencer Rathus is up to his seventh edition of a book titled *Childhood and Adolescence*. In the section about research, Rathus discusses some controversies. He explains the nature-nurture relationship this way: "Researchers are continually trying to sort out the extent to which human behavior

---

106 Ibid, xvi.

is the result of nature (heredity) and of nurture (environmental influences) . . . But today nearly all researchers would agree that nature and nurture play important roles in nearly every area of child development."[107]

Rathus introduces other apparent contradictions in how development occurs but offers no unseen aspects of reality as part of understanding children and adolescents. He ignores self-consciousness and moral agency. He describes the brain as "a sort of a biological computer."[108] He presents the mind only with reference to early pioneers in psychology who tried to develop an understanding of mind that "lies beneath the consciousness"—and this was talking about Freud.[109] Soulness is not mentioned. Living according to our Creator God is not included in any of the discussions about development.

The earlier quote from Dr. Daniel Dalrymple explains why this kind of reductionism does not make sense when we compare it to the observable world. As James K. A. Smith expresses, humans are not simply "brains on a stick" but "embodied agents of desire or love."[110]

What kinds of outcomes happen in education if this reductionist thinking is accepted? Simply put, we look for solutions that look like a formula or recipe. It can sound like, "Follow these steps and

---

107 Spencer A. Rathus, *Childhood and Adolescence: Voyages in Development* (Boston: Cengage Learning, 2016), 128.
108 Ibid, 19.
109 Ibid, 9.
110 James K.A. Smith, *You Are What You Love: The Spiritual Power of Habit* (Ada: Brazos Press, 2016), 3ff.

your class will always behave." Or, as in some parenting books, "Do these six things and have happy children in six weeks!"

While some descriptive research may point to some general patterns of helpful behavior (where "helpful" is defined as "living as our Creator made us to live"), it is the kind of finding that then looks like the practical wisdom of the book of Proverbs in the Bible. For example, social psychologists talk about the need for respect. That is a biblical principle because we are made in the image of God. Similarly, they have spent a good amount of time exploring what is helpful in communication and what is not. Proverbs 12 explains these principles.

This is not to say the Bible contains all truth about such matters, but it is to claim that unless we keep an eye on the eternal aspects of reality (to use an encouragement in Blamires' book), then we cannot see if we are being reductionist and idolatrous. Interestingly, such concerns have also been noted with reference to how psychology (and education) undertake their research.

EXPLORING HOW AN IDOL-BASED WAY OF THINKING CONTRADICTS THE OBSERVABLE FACTS GIVEN TO EVERYONE THROUGH GENERAL REVELATION

Let us for a moment imagine that we are simply the sum total of our nature and nurture. If that was the case, human beings could be studied in the same way we study trees and animals. There would be a certainty about our actions because our thinking would be predetermined by our physical (brain) attributes, which, in turn, could be manipulated by changing the structure of our social context. Our normal brain connections could be manipulated within the limits of genetic predeterminations, and the resulting new behavior would be predictable.

As the quote from Cosgrove indicated, psychology did attempt such behavioristic research in earlier times. Indeed, I was trained in it in the 1970s. However, my lecturers eventually saw that behaviorism simply did not work. Even as an undergraduate student, a couple of instances highlighted this for me. One was when jogging with a colleague who was completing her behaviorist Ph.D. Her research was focused on using behavioral strategies to help people lose weight, which we discussed as we completed our laps around the university oval! I then asked her why she was jogging. Her answer was along the lines of, "Well, it would not be good for a researcher in weight loss to be putting on weight!" We laughed at this.

On reflecting on her self-observation, I made the following comment as a humble undergrad: "But if that helps you lose weight, then why don't you explore that with your research cohort? Why do they get the spinning chairs?" That was her chosen behavioral technique. Our laughter turned to silence, from which we never quite recovered.

Years later, when I was speaking at a national psychology conference, I met a former lecturer who taught us behavioral therapy techniques. He was now lecturing on cognitive behaviorism, or what is now commonly called cognitive behavioral therapy (CBT). This approach looks at how people think as well as act—and "feelings" or "affect" is often included in the review of thinking. I asked my former lecturer why he changed his focus. His reply was short and to the point: "Well, we were wrong." His honesty was refreshing. Why he and others avoided questions from us as students about the reality of our personhood remained unanswered. These are examples of what Pearcey calls checking out reductionist and idolatrous thinking against general revelation. All truth is God's truth, and sometimes, honest descriptions about some aspect of reality can come from many different sources.

Another example of this testing of ideas against reality can be seen in a recent review of how well or poorly different disciplines are using the scientific method. This method is designed to test out ideas that try to understand how physical aspects of reality work. It works best under certain well-prescribed conditions. Stuart Ritchie found that there were systemic problems in satisfactorily meeting these conditions in many disciplines. The issues of concern which he described include a crisis in not being able to undertake appropriate replication of studies: fraud, where a researcher's motives were not committed enough to truth-finding because of competing personal commitments; bias in decision-making about the parameters of the research and in how statistics were manipulated to "hack" for results; negligence in taking enough care in undertaking standard research procedures; hype when results were clearly overstated; and what he called "perverse incentives," in which the professional climate of "publish or perish" resulted in "the natural selection of bad science."[111]

These concerns were all seen in the natural sciences, including medicine, and worst of all, in Ritchie's assessment, in studies into nutrition. What did Ritchie make of studies that involved people? About psychological research, he said, "Psychologists have the unenviable job of trying to understand highly variable and highly complicated human beings . . . difficult, if not impossible, to pin down in a lab experiment . . . Could the sheer complexity of the task make findings in psychology particularly untrustworthy, compared to other sciences . . . There is something to this argument."[112]

Without stating it explicitly, Ritchie is recognizing that the complexity of humans simply do not fit a method designed for investigating physical aspects of reality. Embodied souls simply do not meet the criteria suited to the use of the scientific method. Yet time and time again, you will hear educators say, "But the research says . . . " The problem is that the research that they are quoting is most often reductionist, simplistic, and over-hyped. Ritchie gives an applied example of this. He gives a description of why Carol Dweck's initial research was insufficient for the claims being made about it and then notes, "The risk of such overhyping [of research such as Dweck's] is that teachers and politicians begin to view ideas like mindset as a kind of panacea for education, focusing time and resources on them that might be better spent on dealing with the

---

111 Stuart Ritchie, *Science Fictions: How Fraud, Bias, Negligence and Hype Undermine the Search for Truth*, (Nashville: BH Books, 2020), 194.
112 Ibid, 32.

complex web of social, economic and other reasons that some children fail at school.[113]

I would add that included in this complex web is our embodied soulness, which is indeed unresponsive to the scientific method. Christian Smith came to the same conclusion after carefully explaining why, based on sociological philosophical thinking, we are indeed embodied souls. Smith also notes that the purpose of science "is to understand and explain reality" and that a series of approaches that sought to apply the scientific method to embodied soulness have failed. "We have seen that positivism, reductionism, constructionism, and radical relationalism not only de-center but also often extinguish the person."[114]

Smith, like Ritchie, gives appropriate caution about mistaking correlation with causation. They both describe that much of what is described in such research is the size effect—how big is the sample for the number of variables for which we are controlling? Smith notes how this operational characteristic is consistent with who we are philosophically:

> Variables do not make things happen in the social world. Humans do ... Nor do variables lead to increases and decreases in the values of other variables. Real persons acting in particular contexts in the real world do ... Set against a positivist empiricist backdrop,

---

[113] Ibid, 153.
[114] Christian Smith, *What Is a Person: Rethinking Humanity, Social Life, and the Moral Good from the Person Up* (Chicago: University of Chicago Press, 2011), 234, 265.

> variable social sciences misguidedly thinks that it is attempting to identify lawlike regularities that take the form of observable correlation between events.[115]

Here we see what Pearcey describes—by observing reality carefully, we can see that the reductionist understanding of humanity (nature plus nurture being researched by the scientific manner) does not work. Smith goes on to conclude that we should abandon the "publish or perish" motive in studying humanity "because truth and reality are more important than curriculum vitae and careers."[116]

Ritchie calls for more transparency as we do our research (i.e. not waiting until we complete our research to share about it), even with correlation, because "there's a lot we can learn about how things relate to each other in the world and building up an accurate picture of patterns of correlation is an essential foundation for understanding systems like the brain or society. We need to be awfully careful about how we interpret those correlations, however.[117]

I noted above the example of Dirckx, who is careful both in terms of her physical observations and in her philosophical and biblical contextualisation. She brings together the physical and non-physical aspects of reality in proper relationship (as do Lennox, Swinburne, and others we have reviewed so far). Without such internal coherency, this kind of partial truth that denies non-physical aspects of reality is pretending to be something it is not

---
115 Ibid, 289-90.
116 Ibid, 311.
117 Ibid, 150.

and it will face a consistent difficulty, which is that there is no workable basis to reconcile the idea and reality. As others before me have noted, this is not helpful because a good idea or theory explains reality better than the competing ideas or theories.

NOTING HOW THE IDEOLOGY COLLAPSES IN ON ITSELF BECAUSE IT IS REDUCTIONIST AND REJECTS OBSERVABLE LIFE KNOWLEDGE

Can a nature-plus-nurture construction of reality help us to understand the dynamics of society, where we sometimes see communal good and, at other times, rank evil? If our construct is deficient, we will have difficulty in understanding the good we see in life and the brokenness we also see around us. For example, a number of commentators have described that in the West, we currently struggle with the loss of the concept of sin in the understanding of our social life together. As professor emeritus from Yale, Seymour Sarason, noted some time ago, the result of the loss of the Divine center is a loss for society generally. "Therefore, one must ask what price has been paid in the substitution of the concepts of morals and values for that of sin as a transgression of divine law . . . I would suggest as have many others, that the price we paid was in the weakening of the sense of interconnectedness among the individual, the collectivity and ultimate purpose and meaning of human existence."[118]

More recently, N.T. Wright has described the same pattern through the lens of our current era not being able to explain

---

[118] SB Sarason, "Commentary: The Emergence of a Conceptual Center," *Journal of Community Psychology*, 14 (1986): 405-7.

or discuss the problem of evil. A classic application of this difficulty is in the justice system. Stephen D. Smith has outlined the implications of this in a number of books. He notes that the only way the secularist system works is by "rampant smuggling" of Christian concepts into their constructs.[119] In a later work, he further describes how our era is looking more and more like the ancient paganism of biblical times, and the secularists can only make it work by having a pretence of tolerance—this functional intolerance is how the reductionism is hidden and how the "smuggling" is kept from view. Smith concludes that "this logic of intolerant tolerance is at work in epidemic proportions . . . contemporary progressive tolerance is happy to respect any number of different views—so long that is, as they do not actually proclaim their own truth and hence, expressly or by implication, the error of contrary views.[120]

Does this intolerance apply to how we think about researching the world? The start of this chapter noted some reflections from the anti-theist Richard Dawkins, where even he has admitted that atheistic scientists should be more modest in terms of what they can be certain about and where humility may be a more realistic option—that is, admitting what could not be explained via the scientific method.

The Christian philosopher J. P. Moreland agrees with this sentiment and makes even stronger claims about the humility

---

119 Steven D. Smith, *The Disenchantment of Secular Discourse* (Cambridge: Harvard University Press, 2010), 221.
120 Ibid, 359-60.

that scientists should express in the face of what he describes as "scientism." He explains scientism as the belief that only hard sciences (physical sciences that use the scientific method) can give us true information about reality. The extension of this thinking is that other forms of knowledge are not as valid or true. This then leads to the belief that other sources of information are "neither factual in nature nor subject to rational evaluation."[121]

For example, in psychology, how do we explain the brokenness of humanity—the sin of which Sarason wrote about and the evil which Wright explained? We do not; we ignore it. Outside of Judeo-Christian writings, how then do we also deal with the willfulness of people? In this context, willfulness is the self-centeredness that we naturally carry in our graceless selves. As one education graduate of a state-run university told me, "We were taught to never use consequences in response to poor student behavior—only re-direction and better words." This is the kind of thinking that Dalrymple describes as leading to denying moral responsibility, even after murdering someone. In one case, a woman who murdered her child was given a verdict of manslaughter on "the grounds that she suffered from bad character, known in psychiatric parlance as 'personality disorder.'"[122]

C. S. Lewis described this as pruning a tree branch which happens to be the one on which you were sitting.[123] Without a moral

---

[121] Moreland, 134.
[122] Theodore Dalrymple, *The Knife Went In: Real-life Murderers and Our Culture* (London: Gibson Square, 2018), 188.
[123] C. S. Lewis, *The Abolition of Man*, (Glasgow: Collins Fount Paperbacks, 1943), 49.

frame of reference that is greater than ourselves, we sink to the lowest common denominator of conduct. These ways of describing the inadequacies of reductionist thinking about thinking have had long-term consequences for what we do educationally.

Moreland sums it up this way:

> Over time, a fact/value distinction came about, according to which truth and facts—or in the sciences, empirical knowledge—became the *only* knowledge . . . [that led to colleges believing that they] ought to emphasize "learning how to think" rather than imparting knowledge and wisdom, especially outside the empirical sciences . . . Christian monotheism, having been expelled from the cognitive [thinking] domain, could no longer justify a unified curriculum.[124]

Perhaps a closing comment for this chapter that can capture well the disconnect between ideas about reality and reality itself is the following comment about evolution from philosopher Anthony O'Hear: "There is in Darwinian principles simply no source whence absolute morality can come . . . from a Darwinian perspective, truth, goodness, and beauty and our care for them are very hard to explain."[125]

Given these difficulties in the reductionist paradigms outside of the biblical principles we have explored in this book, how might

---

124 Moreland, 45.
125 Anthony O'Hear, *Beyond Evolution: Human Nature and the Limits of Evolutionary Explanation* (Oxford: Clarendon Press, 2002), 213-14.

Christians explain biblical truths about psychology and education in a more coherent way?

LEARNING TO ARTICULATE THE COHERENCY OF BIBLICAL TRUTHS

In contrast to the difficulties of explaining important human aspects of reality described above, we can quote G. K. Chesterton from a century ago: "Christianity does appeal to a solid truth outside itself: to something which is in that sense external as well as eternal. It does declare that things are really there;[sic] or in other words that things are really things. In this Christianity is at one with common sense; but all religious history shows that this common sense perishes except where there is Christianity to preserve it."[126]

That is, in Christianity, we can have confidence that we have what we need to make sense of seen and unseen aspects of our world in our thinking. Someone who helped our civilizations understand this soon after Christ's ministry on earth was Aurelius Augustine. He responded to charges that Christianity was causing the collapse of society by writing *The City of God*. And he helped those teaching to understand the primacy of Scripture in his *On Christian Teaching*. Augustine was one of the pioneers in explaining to society that the Bible explains reality better, including about how we think, teach, and live.

This early example is what is referred to and promoted in a series of books on academic disciplines from InterVarsity Press. In

---

126 G. K. Chesterton, *The Everlasting Man* (San Francisco: Ignatius Press, 1925), 135.

the preface to the series, Moreland and Beckwith describe several reasons for the need of bringing our faith back into our academic endeavours. They note, "In the early centuries of Christianity, the church presented Jesus to unbelievers precisely because he was wiser, more virtuous, more intelligent and more attractive than Aristotle, Plato, Moses or anyone else."[127]

They propose a series of reasons why it was critical for the Church, through education in particular, to get back to such a position of Christ being introduced to intellectual endeavour wherever it can. They therefore conclude that:

> Christians should do everything they can to gain and teach important and relevant knowledge in their areas of endeavor. At the level appropriate to our station in life, Christians are called to be Christian intellectuals, at home in the world of ideas . . . As Christians, our goal is to make Christian ideas relevant to our subject matter appear to be true, beautiful, good and reasonable to increase the ranking of Christian ideas in the culture's plausibility structure.[128]

That is what we have attempted to do in this book. By focusing on biblical understandings about thinking and the mind, I have attempted to demonstrate that God's revelation in His Word makes more sense of life than the alternatives. When our starting point

---

127 John H. Coe and Todd W. Hall, *Psychology in the Spirit: Contours of a Transformational Psychology* (Christian Worldview Integration Series) (Westmont: InterVarsity Press, 2010), 14.
128 Ibid, 17-21.

is God, we can see purpose in our thinking. When our reference point is Scripture, we have a trustworthy source of life against which we can compare our experiences. Being made in the image of God, we can understand that there is more than physical aspects of reality with which to engage in our thinking. In understanding our brokenness, God's grace in Christ, and the role of faith, we can be reassured that we are made to do the Creator's good (Eph. 2:8-10).

When we further explored the meaning of the mind in Scripture, we also found that thinking is not neutral; it is either drawing us closer to love of God and others or not (excluding the non-intentional instinctual kind of brain-driven responses).

Such a grounding also provided a clearer understanding of our self-consciousness, the relationship between brain and mind, and the development (or not) of character. As part of this understanding, we also noted that in our contemporary world, there has been a shift away from such a transcendent framework for thinking about ourselves to a more individualistic, emotivist, and self-belonging kind of framework. This has been particularly found in the fields of psychology and education.

What then is our starting point? It is grace, through faith.

Conclusion

THINKING AND FAITH

"**DON'T WE THINK MORE SO** that we can understand more, and that leads us to belief?" The Bible college student was checking this out with her pastor.

The pastor's response surprised her. "No, we believe in order to understand." The pastor just let this sentence sit in the following quiet.

"But that doesn't make sense! How can we believe in something if we do not understand the thing in which we are believing?" The student was genuinely confused.

"Ah, I understand. But the Bible teaches us that without God's help, we cannot see anything very clearly at all. So our belief, through faith by grace, is the start to wisdom, which is beyond cleverness of course." The pastor gave a reassuring smile at this point.

The student sat thoughtfully and then said, "Okay. Let's book up some time on this. It is just so different to how I think about how understanding anything works."

Their next session was indeed a long one.

THINKING AND FAITH

Throughout this book, we have seen that the Bible teaches that we cannot split our thinking away from who we are as embodied souls. We have seen passages that clarify that because of sin, our minds need to be renewed; and that only starts by accepting God's mercy. That means we need to "walk by faith, not by sight" (2 Cor. 5:7), to grow in good thinking, or what the Bible calls wisdom.

One of my favorite books about this relationship—between faith and understanding—was written in the era of C. S. Lewis, J. R. R. Tolkien, and Dorothy Sayers. The book is called *Renewing the Mind* and was published in 1949, authored by the theologian and philosopher Roger Hazelton. What fascinates me about the book is that it is both classical and contemporary at the same time.

It is classical because Hazelton sticks with the Bible to make sense of what he explores and also uses the classical work of Augustine to unpack these truths further. What makes his work contemporary is that the issues he covers apply to us at any time, including today.

One of Hazelton's classical statements relates directly to the thesis of this book—that good thinking starts with God: "Difficult as it may be for us, a believing faith in God is all that can save us from our critical intellectual situation . . . For a world without God is a world without truth; indeed it is no world at all, but mere nonsense."[129]

---

129 Roger Hazelton, *Renewing the Mind: An Essay in Christian Philosophy* (New York: The McMillan Company), 23.

For us a Christians, the starting point is God. Without that recognition of reality, our world does not make sense. But God cannot be proven. By His grace, we believe in Him through faith so that we can then do the good He has planned for us (Eph. 2:8-10). This is very uncommon thinking to many in our Western world. We have marginalized God by marginalizing our own "embodied soulness." We do not discuss spirituality in professional contexts, so why would we discuss what our Creator God desires of us?

This book is an encouragement to bring our hearts and souls explicitly back into our thinking in all aspects of our lives, including our professional lives. That exhortation is the "contemporary" nature of Hazelton's work: "Having assumed that God is dead because science, or society, or technical power has killed Him, we invent and manufacture and bow down before other gods—gods in which the mind can find no lasting peace or durable satisfaction."[130] We noted earlier that Augustine explained that the point of living by faith was the "double love" of loving God and loving others more.

Much more recently than Augustine, Andrew Cameron has called us back to this focus. His book, *The Logic of Love,* brings together how our understanding, in faith, can bring us to a clearer understanding of our ethics, which brings our thinking into action toward others. He contends that the mode of God-honoring ethics is love because it is God's love in Christ that rescues us from our "bodies of death" (Rom. 7:24-25). As he notes, "Human love is disordered . . . But the promise of the gospel includes a divine reordering, by the Spirit,

---

130 Ibid, 13.

of love . . . reordered love in two complementary facets forming a theologic [sic] of grace and command."[131]

We see here where good thinking, starting with God, takes us—it is to love. Good thinking is not dry abstraction, nor is it lost sentimentality. It calls us to action to serve others because of the grace and truth that we have received in Christ (1 Peter 4:10-11). This makes sense if we continue to reflect that our thoughts come from the heart (Luke 6:45), as noted at the start of this book. James R. Peters has dwelt on this well in his book, *The Logic of the Heart*. He also helps us understand these connections between our thinking and life by focussing on how our relationship with God is central to who the Bible calls us to be.

For example, he explains that "reason cannot perform this proper function apart from the guidance of the human heart . . . that it is only by cultivating habits of love, properly understood, that we can discover truth about ourselves and make fully rational judgments about the most pressing questions of our age."[132]

Ideologies are the beliefs in which we put our faith. Our role in life as Christians is to worship God. It is through our thinking in fellowship with others, under the teaching of the Word and the guidance of the Holy Spirit that we are able to test our hearts.

What may continue to happen if we allow our thinking about thinking to ignore its soulness and thus the benefit of acting

---

131 Andrew Cameron, *The Logic of Love: Christian Ethics and Moral Psychology* (London: T & T Clark, 2023), 80.
132 James R. Peters, *The Logic of the Heart: Augustine, Pascal, and the Rationality of Faith* (Grand Rapids: Baker Academic, 2009), 17.

within a framework that acknowledges our hearts before God? We are likely to continue to describe aspects of life in a distorted manner because the spiritual aspects of life will be described through a reductionist lens. We will succumb to scientism rather than promote the good use of science. Many authors also suggest that without preserving these biblical basics of personhood and thinking, we will increasingly diminish the dignity of personhood and move toward a less-humane world.

Biblically, we have clearly seen that our distinctly human thinking involves the overflow of the heart, wherein the total aspect of our embodied soulness is seeking God's will and love of others, or it is not. We have seen this through the apostle Paul, who repeatedly describes our thinking processes as bringing glory to God, the Gospel of Christ, and fellowship with others or not. Some examples have included that we are either "hostile in mind" toward God (Col. 1:21), or we are taking "every thought captive to obey Christ" (2 Cor. 10:3-5). Similarly, our thinking is darkened and futile because we push God away (Eph. 4:17-19; Rom. 1:16-32), or we are not surrendering to the patterns of this world by renewing our minds in response to God's mercy (Eph. 4:20-24; Rom. 12:1-2). It is why our thinking can be driven either by our flesh (non-spiritual instincts) or the Holy Spirit (Col. 2:18; Rom. 8:5).

To think well, we need to start with God. Again, quoting Paul, we are made to see both aspects of reality: "as we look not to the things that are seen but to the things that are *unseen*. For the things that are seen are transient, but the things that are *unseen* are eternal"

(2 Cor. 4:18, emphases added). If we do not, we will not know how to love as we think, and we will be like some in Paul's day who let their thinking (knowledge) "puff them up," about which he explained, "If anyone imagines that he knows something [in the "puffed up" way], he does not yet know as he ought to know" (1 Cor. 8:2).

Dirckx summarized it well: "Live with eternity in mind."[133] Lennox's conclusion is the same: "But what about thinking itself? Is it not only important that we think but also how we think ... Man thinks he can become God. But infinitely greater than that is the fact that God thought of becoming human ... we must first repent of the sinful pride that messed up humanity in the first place, and then we need to entrust our lives to Christ as Saviour and follow him as Lord."[134]

Let us think well by starting with God, knowing Him through Christ, and being led by His Holy Spirit. For those of us who desire to take this to all parts of our lives, Hazelton's invitation is still apt for us today:

> Neither world-conforming nor world-condemning but world-transforming is our Christian office . . . Our attitude will therefore be not one of puritan disapproval, monkish avoidance, theological fastidiousness, but that of ministering and sacrificial love ... Let us therefore have this mind in us which was in Jesus Christ our Lord.[135]

---

133 Ibid, 131.
134 Lennox, 225, 227.
135 Ibid, 192.

BIBLIOGRAPHY

Augustine, St. *On Christian Teaching*. R.P.H. Green, trans. Oxford: Oxford University Press, 2008.

Blamires, Harry. *The Christian Mind: How Should a Christian Think?* London: Regent College Publishing, 2005.

Brown, Warren S. and Brad D. Strawn. *The Physical Nature of the Christian Life: Neuroscience, Psychology, and the Church.* Cambridge: Cambridge University Press, 2012.

Brueggemann, Walter. "Covenanting as Human Vocation: A Discussion of the Relation of the Bible and Pastoral Care." *Interpretation* 33. No. 2 (1979):115-29.

Camerson, Andrew. *The Logic of Love: Christian Ethics and Moral Psychology.* London: T & T Clark, 2023.

Chesterton, G. K. *The Everlasting Man.* San Francisco: Ignatius Press, 1925.

Coe, John H. and Todd W. Hall. *Psychology in the Spirit: Contours of a Transformational Psychology (Christian Worldview Integration Series).* Westmont: InterVarsity Press, 2010.

Cosgrove, Mark. *Brain, the Mind, and the Person Within: The Enduring Mystery of the Soul, The.* Grand Rapids: Kregel Academic, 2018.

Cosgrove, Mark. *Psychology Gone Awry.* Westmont: InterVarsity Press, 1982.

Dalrymple, Theodore. *Admirable Evasions: How Psychology Undermines Morality.* New York: Encounter Books, 2015.

Dalrymple, Theodore. *Knife Went In: Real-life Murderers and Our Culture, The.* London: Gibson Square, 2018.

Dirckx, Sharon. *Am I Just My Brain?* Epsom: The Good Book Company, 2019.

Eccles, John. *Mind and Brain: The Many-Faceted Problems.* Icus Books, 1983.

Fee, Gordon. "Getting the Spirit Back into Spirituality." *Life in the Spirit: Spiritual Formation in Theological Perspective (Wheaton Theology Conference Series).* Jeffrey Greenman and George Kalantzis eds. Downers Grove: IVP Academic, 2010.

Fyson, Stephen J. "Character, Oh! Character, Where Art Thou?" *Teach* 10. No. 2 (November 2016): 29-34. https://research.avondale.edu.au/cgi/viewcontent.cgi?article=1324&context=teach.

Glancy, Josh. "How Cancel Culture Clipped Dawkins' Wings." The Weekend Australian Magazine online. November 12, 2021. https://www.theaustralian.com.au/subscribe/news/1/?sourceCode=TAWEB_WRE170_a&dest=https%3A%2F%2Fwww.theaustralian.com.au%2Fweekend-australian-magazine%2Fcancel-culture-clips-richard-dawkins-wings%2Fnews-story%2F665af37f529883923a73134998c27f5c&memtype=anonymous&mode=premium&v21=dynamic-groupb-test-noscore&V21spcbehaviour=append.

Hart, David Bentley. *The Experience of God: Being, Consciousness, Bliss.* New Haven and London: Yale University Press, 2013.

Hazelton, Roger. *Renewing the Mind: An Essay in Christian Philosophy.* New York: The McMillan Company.

Hunter, James Davison. *The Death of Character: Moral Education in an Age Without Good or Evil.* New York City: Basic Books, 2000.

International Webster New Encyclopedic Dictionary of the English Language and Library of Useful Knowledge, The. S.v. "thinking." London: Tabor House, 1972.

Jones, David Gareth. *Our Fragile Brains: A Christian Perspective on Brain Research.* Westmont: Inter-Varsity Press, 1981.

Kanpol, Barry and Mary Poplin, eds. "Blinded by Secular Interpretations of Religious Knowledge." *Christianity and the*

Secular Border Control: The Loss of Judeo-Christian Knowledge (Critical Education and Ethics). Bern: Peter Lang, Inc., International Academic Publishers, 2017.

Koukl, Gregory. *The Story of Reality: How the World Began, How It Ends, and Everything Important That Happens in Between.* Grand Rapids: Zondervan, 2017.

Lennox, John. *2084: Artificial Intelligence and the Future of Humanity.* Grand Rapids: Zondervan Reflective, 2020.

Lewis, C. S. *Abolition of Man, The.* Glasgow: Collins Fount Paperbacks, 1982 edition.

Lewis, C. S. *Abolition of Man, The.* Glasgow: Collins Fount Paperbacks, 1943.

Lukianoff, Greg and Jonathan Haidt. *The Coddling of the American Mind: How Good Intentions and Bad Ideas Are Setting Up a Generation For Failure.* Westminster: Penguin Books, 2018.

Machuga, Ric. *In Defense of the Soul: What It Means to Be Human.* Michigan: Brazos Press, 2002.

MacIntyre, Alasdair. *After Virtue: A Study in Moral Theory, Third Edition.* Notre Dame: University of Notre Dame Press, 2007.

Metcalfe, J. C. *The Bible and the Human Mind.* Fort Worth: CLC Publications, 1996.

Moreland, J. P. *Scientism and Secularism: Learning to Respond to a Dangerous Ideology.* Wheaton: Crossway, 2018.

Nagel, Thomas. *Mind and Cosmos: Why the Materialist Neo-Darwinian Conception of Nature Is Almost Certainly False.* Oxford: Oxford University Press, 2012.

Noble, Alan. *You Are Not Your Own: Belonging to God in an Inhuman World.* Westmont: InterVarsity Press, 2021.

O'Hear, Anthony. *Beyond Evolution: Human Nature and the Limits of Evolutionary Explanation.* Oxford: Clarendon Press, 1997.

O'Hear, Anthony. *Beyond Evolution: Human Nature and the Limits of Evolutionary Explanation.* Oxford: Clarendon Press, 2002.

Packer, J. I. *Knowing God*. London: Hodder and Stoughton, 1973.

Packer, J. I. *Knowing Man*. Englewood: Cornerstone Books, 1979.

Pearcey, Nancy. *Finding Truth: 5 Principles for Unmasking Atheism, Secularism, and Other God Substitutes*. Colorado Springs: David Cook Books, 2015.

Peters, James R. *The Logic of the Heart: Augustine, Pascal, and the Rationality of Faith*. Grand Rapids: Baker Academic, 2009.

Plantinga, Alvin. *Knowledge and Christian Belief*. Grand Rapids: W. B Eerdmans, 2015.

Poplin, Mary Poplin. *Is Reality Secular?: Testing the Assumptions of Four Global Worldviews*. Westmont: InterVarsity Press, 2014.

Rathus, Spencer A. *Childhood and Adolescence: Voyages in Development*. Boston: Cengage Learning, 2016.

Rieff, Philip. *Triumph of the Therapeutic: Uses of Faith After Freud, The*. Wilmington: ISI Books, 2007.

Ritchie, Stuart. *Science Fictions: How Fraud, Bias, Negligence and Hype Undermine the Search for Truth*. Nashville: BH Books, 2020.

Sarason, S. B. "Commentary: The Emergence of a Conceptual Center." *Journal of Community Psychology*, 14 (1986): 405-7.

Smith, Christian. *Moral, Believing Animals: Human Personhood and Culture*. Oxford: Oxford University Press, 2009.

Smith, Christian. *What Is a Person: Rethinking Humanity, Social Life, and the Moral Good from the Person Up*. Chicago: University of Chicago Press, 2011.

Smith, James K. A. *You Are What You Love: The Spiritual Power of Habit*. Ada: Brazos Press, 2016.

Smith, Steven D. *The Disenchantment of Secular Discourse*. Cambridge Harvard University Press, 2010.

Swinburne, Richard. *Mind, Brain, and Free Will*. Oxford: Oxford University Press, 2013.

Szasz, Thomas. *Myth of Mental Illness: Foundations of a Theory of Personal Conduct, The*. New York: Harper Perennial, 2010.

Trueman, Carl. *Rise and Triumph of the Modern Self: Cultural Amnesia, Expressive Individualism, and the Road to Sexual Revolution, The*. Wheaton: Crossway Books, 2020.

Van Inwagen, Peter and Dean Zimmerman, eds. *Persons: Human and Divine*. Oxford: Clarendon Press, 2007.

Van Til, Cornelius. *Introduction to Systematic Theology*. William Edgar, ed. Phillipsburg: P and R Publishing, 2007,

Vitz, Paul C. "Chapter 4: Modern Personality Theories: A Critical Understanding of Personality from a Catholic Christian Perspective." *A Catholic Christian Met-Model of the Person: Integration with Psychology and Mental Health Practice*. Sterling: Divine Mercy University Press, 2020.

Vitz, Paul C. *Psychology as Religion: The Cult of Self-worship*. Grand Rapids: Eerdmans Publishing, 1995.

Watkin, Christopher. *Thinking Through Creation: Genesis 1 and 2 as Tools of Cultural Critique*. Phillipsburg: P and R Publishing, 2017.

Willard, Dallas. *Knowing Christ Today: Why We Can Trust Spiritual Knowledge*. San Francisco: Harper One, 2009.

FOR FURTHER READING

Kittel, Gerhard and Gerhard Friedrich. *Theological Dictionary of the New Testament.* Grand Rapids, Michigan: William B. Eerdmans Publishing Company, 1985.

Hitchens, Peter. *The Rage Against God: How Atheism Led Me to Faith.* Grand Rapids: Zondervan, 2010.

Meyer, S.C. *Return of the God Hypothesis: Three Scientific Discoveries That Reveal the Mind Behind the Universe.* New York, NY: Harper One, 2021.

Smith, Christian. *Atheist Overreach: What Atheism Can't Deliver.* Oxford: Oxford University Press, 2019.

Smith, Christian. *What is a Person: Rethinking Humanity, Social Life, and the Moral Good from the Person Up.* Chicago: Chicago University Press, 2011.

Scruton, Roger. *Fools, Frauds and Firebrands: Thinkers of the New Left.* London: Bloomsbury, 2019.

Smith, S.D. *Pagans and Christians in the City: Culture Wars from the Tiber to the Potomac.* Grand Rapids: William B Eerdmans, 2018.

Trueman, Carl and Ryan T. Anderson. *Strange New World: How Thinkers and Activists Redefined Identity and Sparked the Sexual Revolution.* Wheaton: Crossway, 2022.

ABOUT THE AUTHOR

DR. STEPHEN J. FYSON HAS worked in the helping and teaching professions for over forty years. He was an accredited counseling psychologist for decades and is still teaching and researching in education. Part of the privilege of his work has been helping to establish interest in Christian psychology and Christian teaching in Australia.

For more than thirty-five years, Stephen's focus has been in applying these principles in Christian education at the schooling and tertiary levels. He is currently a part-time Christian education consultant with the Pacific Group of Christian Schools and senior lecturer with Christian Heritage College in their education programs.

He has been supported through all these adventures by his wife of forty-six years, Sandie. His soul is well-fed through time with family (by blood and faith), reading, writing, preaching and teaching, exercising, and engaging with music.

Ambassador International's mission is to magnify the Lord Jesus Christ and promote His Gospel through the written word.

We believe through the publication of Christian literature, Jesus Christ and His Word will be exalted, believers will be strengthened in their walk with Him, and the lost will be directed to Jesus Christ as the only way of salvation.

For more information about AMBASSADOR INTERNATIONAL please visit:

www.ambassador-international.com
@AmbassadorIntl
www.facebook.com/AmbassadorIntl

Thank you for reading this book!

You make it possible for us to fulfill our mission, and we are grateful for your partnership.

To help further our mission, please consider leaving us a review on your social media, favorite retailer's website, Goodreads or Bookbub, or our website.

MORE FROM AMBASSADOR INTERNATIONAL

Like a chef who seasons the meal in such a way that the distinctive flavors of each element is enhanced, Brian Onken invites readers of *More Than a Clever Story* into an invigorating and fresh taste of what Jesus says in His parables. Reading each parable attentive to Jesus' own words and the context in which these stories are found, you'll hear the voice of the Savior in renewed ways. No longer will you think of His parables as clever stories, but you'll find them to be life-giving words from Jesus.

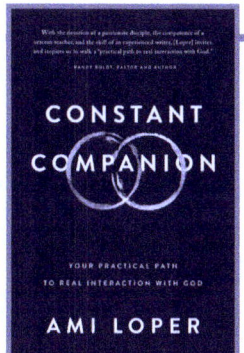

Every human heart longs to be truly known and deeply loved. Each person has a God-given longing for fulfillment and a sense of belonging that is met only in a relationship with God. But does God really want a relationship with you? Yes, and He demonstrates His desire for that over and over again in Scripture. *Constant Companion* shows readers how to get past feelings of unworthiness, unwillingness, and other distractions and how to listen to God's voice through the practices of meditation, prayer, and Scripture-reading.

Most of us know Who Jesus is and would admit He was a good and kind Teacher while here on earth. But He is so much more—He is our Savior and God and worthy of all our worship. Through an in-depth study into the book of Hebrews, Joshua West and Gary Wilkerson take apart each verse, drawing the reader to a closer look at the Man Who lived here on earth for a short time and then became our Sacrifice to save us from our sins and live with us eternally in Heaven with Him. If you are searching for something more from God, dive into this study and drink in the jaw-dropping beauty of our Jesus.

www.ingramcontent.com/pod-product-compliance
Lightning Source LLC
LaVergne TN
LVHW051500070426
835507LV00022B/2860